D1094439

WRITING

ARTICLES

THAT SELL

An idea arrives without effort;
a form can only be wrought out by patient effort.

—HENRY VAN DYKE

WRITING
ARTICLES
THAT SELL

Louise Boggess

Englewood Cliffs, N.J.   **PRENTICE-HALL, INC.**

PRINTED IN THE UNITED STATES OF AMERICA

97040—B&P

To Bill

my husband and favorite critic

How This Book Can Help You Sell Your Articles

The purpose of this book is to show you how to write salable magazine articles. If you are willing to work and will follow the instructions given, you can, without a doubt, write an article that sells.

Unless someone guides you in the study of professional writing techniques, you can waste years struggling. By learning the basic patterns and simple techniques explained and illustrated in this book, and by putting them to work for you, you can eliminate those wasted years.

Most books on writing explain technique by analyzing a published article and working backward to the idea. This book shows you how to develop your idea step by step through the basic techniques into an article the way the writer naturally works.

7

As you move from the simple informative piece to the more complex fictional article, all techniques are explained and illustrated as you need them, one at a time. Hence this presentation will benefit the professional writer as well as the amateur and the beginner.

This method of writing articles has been tested in my classes and has been proven time after time with sales. Not only can you write and sell an article but you can do it again and again.

Louise Boggess

College of San Mateo
San Mateo, Calif.

Contents

9

WRITING
ARTICLES
THAT SELL

1.

Ideas
Finding and Testing Them

At a writers' conference, a young housewife confided, "I want to write magazine articles."

"Which kind?" I asked.

"Is there more than one kind?" She looked surprised.

Like many amateur writers, she is unaware that the word *article* includes a broad field of choices between the *factual* and the *fictional* piece. These two categories include nine basic types of article which vary in length from 500 to 5000 words; in subject matter, from baking a cake to exploring the jungles of South America; and in market, from religious to men's adventure magazines. In fact, some articles are so fictionalized in treatment that you easily mistake them for short stories.

Most likely, this housewife will follow the example of other newcomers to writing and resort to the trial and error method which makes the apprenticeship unnecessarily long and discouraging. The quicker and more successful method of learning to write any type of article is a step-by-step procedure which professional writers use. The first step is finding a salable idea. An *idea* is an emotional reaction to a person, place, or situation which urges you to write. Salable ideas are all around you if you know how to find them.

FINDING IDEAS

To find ideas, you must become perceptive to people, places, and situations. Any reaction or experience you are unable to dismiss from your mind is most likely a salable idea. The most available source of ideas is your own experience.

1. *Your Experiences*

A mother of six children protested, "My experiences are so ordinary that no one would want to read them." With a perceptive mind, she discovered that readers are people like herself and that ordinary ideas frequently sell better than unusual ones.

With this new outlook, she found several ideas to convert into articles. Before she went to the hospital for an operation, she efficiently organized the children to carry on the household routine. No outside help was required. How she accomplished this made one article. On another occasion she organized a babysitters' cooperative at her church, and this provided material for another article. Search your daily life for ideas. Probably you have discovered some short cuts to save time in doing household chores or have experimented with cheaper and better ways to make home repairs. Have you improvised a successful plan for getting acquainted in a new neighborhood, church, or community? Surely, you know an interesting personality who does worthwhile work in your community. Perhaps you have made an adjustment to a serious illness or feel strongly about a controversial issue. Any of these reactions suggest an idea for a profitable article.

Childhood memories also stimulate ideas for articles. Remember the uncle who was always going to strike it rich on some wild scheme and wanted your family to finance him? You may recall the good old days when families stayed in one town, and excitement was going for a soda at the corner drug store. Search your memory for wonderful nostalgic ideas.

Have notebook and camera ready for special events scheduled in your life. Such preparation before vacation trips, a controversial meeting with the school board, or a church fund drive results in ideas for salable articles.

Let each day provide you with new ideas. As you exhaust your own experiences, borrow those of your friends and neighbors, or even of strangers.

2. *Experiences of Others*

Encourage your friends and associates to share their experiences with you. At a dinner party, a woman related how disgusted she was with another secretary who shared her car pool. From this conversation came a sale on the types of secretaries to exclude from a car pool.

At every opportunity, observe the activities of others. A writer who supports a family of five selling articles to trade journals and business publications has trained himself to find ideas wherever he goes. When he made a purchase at a drug store, he saw a window display worthy of an article. From an afternoon visit with a neighbor who was building storage cabinets in the garage, he found three ideas to develop into salable articles: how to build storage cabinets in a garage, what new materials are available for do-it-yourself builders, and economical short cuts in construction.

Your experiences and those of others are original sources which have not been used previously. After original sources are depleted, search for stimulation from published articles.

3. *Newspapers and Magazines*

Keep your scissors handy as you read a newspaper. Any information in a straight news story of a newspaper becomes public domain after twenty-four hours. Public domain does not include newspaper stories, columns, or press releases marked "copyright." To take this information without giving credit is plagiarism, and permission of the copyright owner *must* be obtained.

A news story on a business firm hiring its first lady truck driver was developed into a personality sketch for a trucking magazine. An item on how an overcrowded school converted a bus into a classroom became another salable article. Clip the items and contact the proper authority for more facts.

Frequently a news story discusses plans in the developmental stage. A school decides to try an experimental method of instruction. Medical research reveals a new treatment for a disease or an experiment with a new drug. A civic organization takes on a new community project. A person exhibits great courage. Collect more information as these stories develop.

Newspapers often suggest related ideas. An accident with a firecracker inspired an article on "Safety with Fireworks." A series of short articles on raids by raccoons led to a humorous sketch on the habits of raccoons.

One sentence in a magazine article can send your thoughts along an entirely different subject. "Too many young people are sitting life out" was a sentence in a magazine article which developed into a teenage piece on how to get into the traffic of life. Often the approach or slant the author uses in an article makes you feel he is biased or too unrealistic in presenting the facts. Why not write your side of the subject and send the article to that magazine or its competitor?

In addition to reading for ideas, you can discover them while listening to the radio or watching television.

4. *Television and Radio*

Listen to speeches, plays, and even commercials on television and radio. Advertisements are wonderful stimulators of ideas because creative people have packed reader identity ideas into concentrated forms. The announcer tells you about tea. Instantly, you begin to wonder how, where, and when people came to use tea or iced tea.

A newscast is another rich source of ideas because it serves as an index to the newspaper, pointing out the most interesting and dramatic events. Doing a follow-up on a newscast eliminates detailed reading of the newspaper in your search for ideas.

A play on television or radio may turn your thoughts toward parent-teenager relations or marital problems. A documentary often inspires research on a related subject.

Challenging radio and television programs are not always timed to fit your convenience, but an abundance of printed material is available for your leisure reading at any time.

5. *Printed Material*

The mailman delivers ideas to you every day. News, publicity, and promotional letters frequently contain good ideas for articles. In an aviation newsletter, one writer read a personal experience story on the first pilots to fly the mail. He contacted the author for more information and sold the article to a national market.

Get on the mailing lists of your congressman, social and business organizations, or your church. Newsletters from big companies tell of recent research in their special fields. A letter to the public relations department will put your name on the mailing list.

If you own stock in a company, the annual report discusses new products and services. The stuffers that come with your utility bills or those of department stores tell about new products and interesting events. Government booklets, on which there are no copyrights, are excellent sources of researched information and cost only a nominal fee.

A catchy phrase, "dreams money can buy," in an advertisement on a theater program challenged one writer to list and humorously discuss such items in an article. Another source of untapped information is a college library where a graduate student is required to file his thesis or dissertation. One of these may contain the idea for your next sale.

Very likely you can think of other printed sources which will contribute ideas.

6. *Editors*

After you have made several sales to an editor, he will send you ideas. One editor pointed out that California was doing an excellent job in school construction. From this idea developed a series of articles on school plants. Another editor of a home service magazine casually remarked that California led the nation in modern home construction. This idea developed another series of articles on home planning in California.

7. *Writing Classes and Conferences*

Writing articles is not a lonely profession but one which demands contact with people. Writing classes or workshops offer excellent opportunities to brainstorm ideas. Colleges and universities, through extension courses and public school adult programs, are providing writing classes for the smaller as well as the larger communities. Classes are advantageous in that the teacher, as a rule, is a professional writer who gives valuable instruction in technique and also directs the criticism.

For the beginning writer who is completely isolated, many universities offer correspondence courses in writing techniques. Usually, the director is a professional writer.

Writing conferences are held mostly during the summer in all parts of the United States. These help beginners by stimulating ideas, giving valuable information on the writing craft, and providing contact with editors and professional writers. Friendship with these writers will eventually get you a recommendation to a good agent.

8. Agent

Many unsuccessful writers feel that all they need to sell is a good agent. This is wishful thinking. A *reputable* agent takes only writers who are selling and who probably will continue to produce. Unless you have a salable article, an agent can do nothing for you. The final chapter instructs on how to submit your manuscript directly to an editor without an agent.

The best way to get an agent is to sell regularly. Then you can contact an agent or ask a professional writer to recommend you to his agent. Occasionally, an agent will contact you. After you have worked with an agent, he will know what you write best and be on the alert to make new contacts for you. An agent is most valuable with book contracts.

Selecting Your Ideas

To demonstrate how to write the various types of articles, I will select five ideas to develop. You will learn professional writing techniques faster if you will find five similar ideas. Learning is doing, and these techniques become yours only if you put them to work for you. By doing the suggested practice at the end of each chapter, you will have nine different ideas ready to put into first draft copy.

1. A General Idea

A general idea is broad in scope and at the same time provides essentially negative and affirmative sides. You will develop this idea into four types of factual article. My general idea for these developments is "guarantees or warranties." Other general ideas are: insurance, discount houses, team teaching, or junior colleges.

2. An Abstract Idea

This idea will demonstrate the technique of the inspirational article. To find this idea, list a number of abstract subjects: giving, hope, generosity, courage, bravery, or criticism. From one of these, pose a problematical question. What is the courageous heart? Who is the generous person? How do you acquire a hopeful mind? This will help you find an inspirational idea. I will develop "the worried mind."

3. An Idea for a Personality Sketch

For the personality sketch, choose any interesting individual of your acquaintance or one you can interview, well-known or otherwise. The only criterion is that this person has made or is making a worthwhile contribution to humanity. My sketch deals with an old-time journalist.

4. A Personal Experience Idea

Search your life for an exciting adventure, a challenging experience with which the reader can identify himself, or a dramatic event in which you participated. The adventure pertains to exploring or taking part in sports. The reader can identify with such experiences as changing jobs or professions, adopting children, going back to school. Perhaps you took part in a daring rescue, had a freak accident, or adapted to a physical disability. If your experiences are too mild, relate that of a personal friend, but in first person as he told it to you. My personal experience idea concerns a friend who went to college after she was thirty-five.

5. A Nostalgic Idea

From your past find a poignant memory for a nostalgic idea. Perhaps you recall your first train trip, the senior class play in which you were the lead, a Fourth of July barbecue, a family reunion, or the wedding of a favorite teacher. You may regret the passing of old-fashioned hay rides or old-time tent shows. My nostalgic idea pertains to the time my father built a cyclone cellar.

When you have put your receptive mind to work and found five parallel ideas, the next step is to test their salability.

Successful writers have learned to test ideas for certain basic characteristics before they waste time trying to put them into article form. The procedure is very simple.

1. *Enthusiasm*

Enthusism begins with liking your idea. In any factual or fictional article you write, your personal reactions are projected to the reader. When you write on a subject you dislike or one which does not hold your interest, the reader knows and so does the editor. A good rule to follow is to write on subjects which generate your enthusiasm.

Being enthusiastic also means believing in your idea. A salesman finds it difficult to sell a product in which he has lost faith. You will have difficulty selling an article which lacks your whole-hearted confidence.

Enthusiasm challenges you to explore your idea thoroughly. The more you research, the stronger is your urge to put this collected information into an article and share it with the reader.

2. *Message*

Whether you write a factual or fictional article, you must personalize the general subject by giving your specific reactions. To personalize the general subject of cyclone cellar, you state that it brings people together for better understanding—your specific reaction. Express your reaction in one pithy statement, called a theme, premise, or capsule sentence. This message to the reader not only expresses your individual opinion but also promises verification of your attitude.

A general idea for a factual piece usually contains four or five strong capsule sentences from which you can write the same number of articles. The way you state the capsule sentence determines the type of factual article. Later chapters discuss the capsule sentence in detail.

In the fictional article, the statement of the message has no relation to the type of article, but you merely summarize what the events of the story prove. You may state it in different ways, but you select the strongest message. The message in the fictional article is a *theme*.

3. Conflict

In writing the factual article, you state a fact, then relate an example. The incidents illustrating the facts provide the conflict in the factual article. When you have trouble illustrating an idea, you probably need more research. Illustrations are discussed in Chapter 7.

Conflict in the fictional article comes from the central character conquering the adversities he meets in trying to accomplish his goal. The individual who has no struggles will not interest the editor or the reader. Chapter 13 discusses plotting the fictional article.

4. Reader Identity

An article offers the reader either self-identity or escape. He may compare the material to his own life and find a common ground of understanding. Readers who wish to escape from a humdrum routine prefer to read about people, places, or situations they will never encounter in their own life. The factual article appeals to the realist while the fictional reaches both the realist and the dreamer. An idea which appeals to both is excellent, for this enlarges the number of readers and wins the editor's approval with a check.

5. Market

The amateur writes and then searches for a market, but the professional finds the market and then writes. For a quick check on markets, Poole's *Index to Periodical Literature* at most libraries lists printed articles by title, magazine, date, volume, and page number.

Look under the key word, for example "guarantee." Before you decide there is nothing in print on your idea, try different phrasings or key words, such as "warranty." An idea which has not been developed into an article is either new material or has taboos.

A *taboo* is a ban editors put on certain subjects as being in poor taste for their magazines or contrary to their basic beliefs. Catholic markets taboo divorce. Trade journals for writers list taboos in the market information sections. Some editors include taboos on requirement sheets they clip to your manuscript as a rejection slip. Since taboos are constantly changing, file such ideas so designated, for they may become acceptable later.

From Poole, list the magazines which have published articles related to your idea and read these. Your library usually has back copies on file. Add to this list from market news in magazines for writers until you have six possibilities. Further discussion on markets appears in the final chapter.

6. *Plus Value*

In today's competitive market, the beginner must compete with the professional. To meet this competition, develop a plus value in each article you write.

A *plus value* lifts your article from the ordinary by giving it an extra quality or spark which catches the editor's attention. Your plus value may change with each article, or you can develop a quality which puts a signature on any piece you write. A stimulating style, faultless research, timeliness of subject, or excellent continuity are all plus values.

Striving for perfection and consciously checking to see if you have given the best of yourself to the article is the sure way to achieve plus value.

SUGGESTED PRACTICE

Writing salable articles requires self-discipline to follow instructions and conscious practice to make the basic techniques work for you. To profit most from this book, test each of your five ideas and put them on file cards as demonstrated below. Since you alone know your enthusiasm, only five of the tests will appear on the cards.

1. *Guarantees*

> *Message:* Everyone should learn about guarantees.
> Correct procedure gets results. Guarantees are valu-

able. Do companies stand behind guarantees?

Conflict: Guarantees tested on watch, refrigerator, car, raincoat, washing machine, electric blanket, bridge cards, floors of a house, dress material, bamboo drapes, lamps with brass base, and others.

Reader Identity: Anyone who has purchased or plans to purchase a product carrying a guarantee.

Market: Digest, home service, women's magazines.

Plus Value: Technical knowledge gained in using guarantees.

2. The Worried Mind

Message: Get rid of your worries.

Conflict: Contrast person who worries with one who does not.

Reader Identity: Anyone who worries.

Market: Digest, religious, women's magazines.

Plus Value: Self-help for the reader.

3. Old-Time Journalist

Message: He practices freedom of the press.

Conflict: An editor who sets his own standards of newsworthy items and does not spare his personal opinions.

Reader Identity: An editor who does what others only dream of doing.

Market: Digest, men's magazine.

Plus Value: The character of the man.

4. *Personal Experience*

Message: Happiness is the reward for doing.

Conflict: A widow who did not finish high school decides to go to college so she can support her two daughters.

Reader Identity: Anyone who has gone to school or who has the responsibility of supporting a family.

Market: Digest, educational journal, women's magazines.

Plus Value: The mother's courage in solving her problems.

5. *Father and the Cyclone Cellar*

Message: A helping hand restores faith in oneself.

Conflict: A father of six decides to build a cyclone cellar over his wife's protests and gives men who are failures a renewed confidence in themselves.

Reader Identity: The family situation and the small town setting.

Market: Digest, religious, women's magazines.

Plus Value: The setting, the times, and the banker situation.

Note that only the general classification or group of markets is given rather than the specific magazine. On *your* card, you will list the specific magazine in the group.

2.

Choosing
a Viewpoint

Viewpoint identifies the relation of the author to the material and provides the emotional coloring. How emotionally you write depends upon whether you relate the facts objectively or subjectively.

OBJECTIVE VIEWPOINT

An objective viewpoint is an unbiased reporting of facts. After you cover all facets of the subject, the reader is free to draw his own conclusions and apply the information any way he chooses. The use of action verbs and adjectives provides the emotional coloring. Primarily, the emotion comes from presenting the facts in a thought provoking sequence.

Encyclopedias are written from the objective viewpoint. With the exception of straight news stories or fillers, such as household hints or recipes, few articles use the objective viewpoint. Since most readers wish to identify in some way with the article material, more and more short informative pieces are written subjectively.

SUBJECTIVE VIEWPOINT

In a subjective viewpoint, the reader identifies with the author and accepts his reactions on the subject. As author, you present only one side of the subject—your side; hence all articles are written with a single viewpoint.

Maintaining a single viewpoint keeps the reader identifying with you or your subject and accepting your opinions and conclusions as correct. Your material will assist you in selecting the best single viewpoint.

1. *Single Major Character*

When you the author are the chief participant in the events of either the factual or the fictional article, employ the single major character viewpoint, first person. *Person* refers to the personal pronoun which identifies the viewpoint.

> I parked the car in the empty stall at the garage and nodded to the mechanic. He shuffled toward me, sipping a cup of coffee.
>
> "Battery trouble again?" he questioned.
>
> "I'm disgusted," I admitted. Everyone has a new battery go bad occasionally, but this was the third one for me in two months.

The example shows the author in the first person, major character viewpoint, putting a guarantee into action. To assume the major character viewpoint, you must know who you are and what facet of your total personality to emphasize. Everyone has a number of identities. Suppose you are a parent, lawyer, and president of a civic club.

When you write an article on the rearing of six children, you emphasize the fact that you are a parent. Your other identities are not mentioned because they have little relation to the subject. If you write on needed revisions in state laws, you stress your legal training. As president of the civic club, you show why people should beautify the town. You choose the facet of your total identity which convinces the reader you have something worthwhile to say on the subject.

Do not assume an identity which is not your own unless you are collaborating with the person in authority and doing an as-told-to article. On the other hand, you need not be a lawyer to object to a bad law—any citizen can do this. In brief, write from your own experience as much as possible. Any time you go beyond the realm of your own experience, notify the reader by quoting the authority.

Some writers feel that the first person sounds too egotistical, so they create a mythical character and rely on the third person, single major character, to convey the information.

> Jim Wilson had never used a guarantee in his life, but he had no choice. He walked purposefully toward the clerk at the appliance counter, then stopped. He fumbled through several pockets before he found a

folded piece of paper, his guarantee on the lawn mower.

Jim will not think in the *I* but always in the third person *he*. The drawback to this type of single major character viewpoint is that it gives a fictional coating, and the reader doubts the veracity of your facts.

2. *Single Minor Character*

In the single minor character viewpoint, you are not the major participant, but you are on scene to observe and report what happens.

> My father spread the impressive design of where to locate the cyclone cellar on the dining table. I snuggled close to him while my brothers and sisters clustered around the table.
>
> "Here's the windmill," my brother shouted.
>
> "I've found the cistern, this circle," my sister added. I wanted to find a landmark, too.
>
> "Where's the rose garden?" I asked as Mother joined us.
>
> Father cleared his throat. Mother gasped and pushed him aside. "My rose garden. That fool has located the cellar in the middle of my rose garden!"
>
> I crawled under the table, but Father took care of the situation. "Hold your temper until you hear my plans for your rose garden."

In this example, Father is the major character, but the *I* observes what happens and emotionally reports it to the reader.

In this age of cooperation, much experimental work is the result of a team. If you are a member of a team, you make the team and its work the major interest of the article but tell the story from your viewpoint as a minor participant. Likewise, you are a minor character narrator when you observe the work of such a group and report it to the reader.

3. *Implied Viewpoint*

With some articles you find that identifying yourself as either the major or minor participant will detract from the importance of the subject or confuse the reader.

> Ed Harvey devised his own journalism rules. He found that the most appropriate reward for his largest and oldest advertiser was to give him the best spot in the newspaper. In spite of protest and criticism, the advertisement occupied the center of the front page.

While the reader realizes that someone provides the information and the emotional reactions, there is no identity of author by personal pronoun. Such identity takes the spotlight from Ed Harvey, the major character.

The implied viewpoint takes the reader on scene to observe the situation but shows only what will support your personal reactions to the subject. This type of viewpoint is difficult to master but gets better pay checks from the editor because of the strong reader identity.

4. *Single Viewpoint—Dual Pronoun*

Information in the factual articles reaches the reader quicker if presented in a conversational or chatty tone. You achieve this tone by using two personal pronouns. The *I* of the author talks with the *you* of the reader.

> You have experienced one of those days when every-thing went wrong. You had a flat tire and arrived late at the office. Then you discovered that you'd left your glasses on the dresser at home, and working with figures gave you a headache. My day went that way, too.

In the above example the *I* provides the emotional reaction for the *you,* but the *I* and the *you* are brought into the action.

Reverse the combination and open the article in the *I,* transferring quickly to the *you.*

> When I bought the tires, I thought I read all the fine print on the guarantee. Evidently, my mind did not react to one provision restricting the guarantee to operation in certain states. When the tire went bad, I was in the wrong state.
>
> No doubt, you felt confident that you knew what the guarantee covered only to discover a shocking clause which nullified the company's responsibility.

In like manner, you can alternate between *we* and *you.* *We* sounds less accusing when you say, "we are all guilty," including yourself, than "you are guilty," seemingly excluding yourself. Write the article in the second person, then come back and substitute *we* at points which sound too dictatorial.

A most effective combination is the implied *I* with the stated *you*.

> Before you buy a product, read the guarantee carefully. If you do not understand some of the provisions, ask for an interpretation.

In the above example, the *I*, implied, tells *you*, the reader, what to do. The use of two personal pronouns in the fictional article is a novelty rather than an accepted practice.

The fictional article confines itself to three viewpoints: single major character, single minor character, or implied. No matter which single viewpoint you choose, you can enter the mind of only one person, you the author. When you have chosen the correct viewpoint, your next step is to learn how to convey your individual reactions through this device to the reader.

PROJECTING THE VIEWPOINT

Your reactions and emotions reach the reader faster if he has a mental picture of you. As you present the subject, you also sketch yourself as the author viewpoint. The devices are simple.

1. *Your Words*

What you say to the reader, your choice of words and your opinions must characterize you. A simple direct style gives one picture while one decorated with numerous adjectives projects another. Short sentences as compared to long ones offer another contradictory picture. Study your subject and carefully select words which will project your chosen image to the reader.

Any dialogue in an illustration shows the type of person you are. In this example, the *I* speaks with determination.

> The adjuster scowled.
> "You'd only be wasting time to take this matter to the president of the company," he warned.
> "It's not a matter of time but of principle," I assured him forcefully.

2. *Your Actions*

You may speak one way but act another. Usually, actions have more meaning for the reader, so wisely choose your actions and favorably impress the reader.

> When the man behind the counter doubted that the electric blanket was defective, I pushed it toward him. "Test it."
> He seemed reluctant to pick it up. "It will take fifteen minutes at least."
> I shrugged and sat down in a nearby chair.

Again, you see determination.

3. *Your Thoughts*

The thoughts of other characters in the piece are surmised from actions or words, but the author's are shared with the reader. These thoughts relate the problem and conflicts of the viewpoint.

> I listened without actually hearing, and yet I somehow grasped the meaning of the situation. I could not enter college without high school credits; yet it was impossible for me, close to forty, to go back to high school. I must find another way to enter college.

By letting the reader know exactly what you feel in your thoughts, you establish your character image as well as quick identity for the reader.

4. *Reactions of Others*

The reaction of others to your words and actions projects your image to the reader.

> The man began to fill out the form. "No matter how much you insist, all I can do is recommend a replacement."

These four devices are interwoven to project the one image which will lead your reader to believe the facts of your article.

SUGGESTED PRACTICE

Choose the best viewpoint for each of your five ideas by writing several paragraphs of each type illustrated.

3.

| Using
| the Factual Formula |

Professional writers use a basic formula to develop an idea into a salable article. A *formula* is a general outline which helps you organize your material effectively. As expected, the formula for the factual article differs from that of the fictional, explained in Chapter 13. At first you must work consciously to develop an idea through either formula. With continuous practice, applying the formula to an idea becomes almost a reflex.

The factual formula consists of six parts: hook, capsule sentence, authority, development, conclusion, and twist.

HOOK

A *hook* is the bait at the beginning of the article to catch the reader's attention. It varies in length from one sentence in the 500-word article to several paragraphs in the 5000-word. To catch the reader's attention, it must contain certain elements.

1. *Reader Reaction*

You predetermine the reaction you want from your reader. If you wish your reader to think, the hook contains a reasonable but challenging thought. Perhaps you want your reader to act. Then you hook him with action he can easily duplicate. To get him to react emotionally, you set the mood with a short anecdote, a dramatic or nostalgic incident. Therefore your basic reactions are: to think, to act, or to react in some defined emotion which varies with the subject matter.

2. *Viewpoint*

The hook establishes the viewpoint of the article. You want the viewpoint in the opening sentence.

3. *Subject*

The hook always introduces the general subject of the article and hints at the author's individual opinion or reaction as expressed in the capsule sentence.

Since the hook creates the reader reaction, introduces the viewpoint, and states the subject, practically every word performs a function. Practice, however, makes the hook less difficult to write. The next chapter covers the actual technique of writing the hook for both the factual and the fictional article.

Capsule Sentence

As soon as you attract the attention of the reader, your next step is to convince him that you have an important message for him. You express this briefly in the capsule sentence. This sentence not only convinces the reader that he will enjoy reading this article but it also carries the key to the development.

If the subject matter is news, as in recent scientific or medical research, you may need a statement or two after the hook to lead gradually into the capsule sentence. Any time the reader is already familiar with the subject, one sentence is sufficient.

Write your capsule sentence until you have the best combination of words to get strong reader interest and at the same time express your personal view on the subject. Study the capsule sentences on your idea card for the factual article and see if you can improve them.

Author's Authority

The reader must know at all times that you have the ability and experience to write about your chosen subject. The way you show your authority varies.

1. *Location*

The location of an article in a specific section of a magazine implies authority. An article appearing in a section on gardening is sufficient proof of the author's authority. The editor would not have published the piece unless he had checked on the author's qualifications. In writing for trade or professional journals, you need not state your qualifications.

2. *Statement*

In articles based on your own experience, one sentence is sufficient: "For the past ten years, I have had numerous opportunities to use my guarantees on a wide assortment of products and with varying results." This simple statement tells your authority and your identity.

3. *Arrangement of Facts*

In most short articles, the presentation of facts and illustrations in a logical and plausible style establishes your authority. The facts speak for themselves.

4. *Research*

A carefully researched article dealing with a controversial subject requires that you tell the reader where you found the facts, how extensively you researched them, and why you drew such conclusions. Even then, you will need to scatter sentences throughout the article to remind the reader of this careful research.

5. *Blurb or Footnote*

When a person, especially qualified to discuss a subject, writes for a general magazine, the blurb under the title or a footnote states his qualifications. The information relates whether he has written books on the subject or has had practical experience in the field.

6. *As-Told-To Authority*

Writers frequently sell articles based on the experiences of another person. The byline on the article carries the name of the person with the experience and as-told-to the author. Upon submitting this type of article, include a letter to the editor containing the consent of the person involved.

DEVELOPMENT

The *development* is the body of the article and consists of factual points and illustrations. Three-fourths of the wordage in an article is allotted to the development.

1. *Factual Points*

Think of your article as one side of a debate and list the various points which will prove your capsule sentence. To win the reader to your way of thinking, all points must relate to and elaborate the capsule sentence.

In developing the idea that a guarantee is valuable, the following statements are arranged in a logical and chronological order to make the reader think:

> Guarantees give information on the minimum life expectancy of products.
>
> They save money on future repairs and replacements.
>
> They prove the reliability of the company which made the product.
>
> They make everyone a more cautious buyer.

The number of points to develop depends upon the meatiness of the capsule sentence. Five strong points are better than ten weak statements. Avoid the use of numerous subheads under a major point as such arrangement confuses the reader and weakens the argument.

The desired reader reaction also affects the arrangement of the discussion points. To make the reader think, arrange the points in logical sequence. Comparison or contrast stimulates thinking, too. Building to a dramatic crisis as well as alternating between logical and shocking statements moves the reader emotionally.

The simplest way to choose the correct sequence is to put each point on a small file card. Try various arrangements of these cards until you find the most effective one for your reader reaction and the presentation of the material.

2. *Illustrations*

An illustration shows the reader what your statement means and gives him time to absorb the fact. An article which presents one fact after another overpowers the mind of the reader, and he retains little. He may stop reading because the material appears too difficult for his comprehension. Articles that sell keep the reader reading until the last word.

An article which states a fact and illustrates, repeating this arrangement throughout the development, makes interesting facts dull. State a fact and illustrate, then illustrate and conclude with the fact, or sandwich the fact into the middle of the illustration. Variety in the arrangement of the development paces the article.

To accomplish this variety, write your article stating the fact and illustrating. When you have done the first draft, go back and re-arrange according to the above suggestion.

Likewise, vary the technical devices of your illustrations. More difficult points for discussion may need a scene or several incidents for illustration while another statement requires only a quotation from a well-known authority. Chapter 7 discusses in detail how to illustrate an article.

When you have discussed and illustrated all of your points, proceed to the conclusion.

CONCLUSION

A conclusion briefly summarizes the development and restates the capsule sentence in different words. This restatement follows the old literary essay which always related the opening statement to the final conclusion.

Most articles wind up quickly. The conclusion is rarely more than one paragraph with one exception. When an article criticizes an existing practice and demands reform, the reader expects the author to suggest a feasible remedy or plan. In this type of critical article, the conclusion is nearer in length to the development.

TWIST

The beginning dictates the twist which varies in length from one sentence to a short paragraph. Certainly you do not open indicating that you are a lawyer and close with a picture that reveals you to be a housewife. Neither do you open humorously and close with a shocking, dramatic scene. The twist always repeats the mood of the hook.

There are three basic ways to twist an article.

1. *To Think*

In urging the reader to think, you-the-author must speak personally to him. The material suggests the forcefulness. If you want to pressure the reader to use his guarantee, urge immediate action:

> So your dryer keeps blowing fuses. Use your warranty today. Tomorrow may be too late.

The twist on the article may only caution the reader.

> A warranty is your insurance against costly repairs or replacements. Use it!

The urgency for immediate action is no longer there.

2. *To Chuckle*

Humor is a good device to make the reader remember the serious message of the article. When your style is light but with serious undercurrents, an amusing anecdote or a wise saying is a good exit.

Since the example idea deals strictly with using your guarantee when a product develops defects, end with a woman whose purchases have developed no defects.

> May you be like the woman who eagerly listened to my experiences on guarantees. "How I envy you," she said. "I can't wait for my new refrigerator to break down so I can use my guarantee."

3. *To Sob*

The sob ending applies more to the fictional article. Imagine yourself in a theater, the star speaks the final dramatic words, the curtain slowly closes. A lump forms in your throat while you sit there a second to savor the final emotion. That's the effect you want to produce at the end of a dramatic first person experience, a personality sketch, or a sentimental nostalgic piece.

> Ed Harvey stared at the award for an intense moment. "This doesn't belong to me. I never took a journalism lesson in my life."
>
> "Maybe not," the nationally known correspondent agreed, "but you've taught a number of graduate journalists the meaning of freedom of the press."

A good habit to form is to write the twist as soon as you finish the hook of your article. Not only will you know your final destination but you will overlap the mood of the hook.

Suggested Practice

Write examples of the three types of twist and clip them to the idea card with which they will be used.

4.

It's the Hook
That Gets the Editor

The hook directs the reader's attention to the subject matter discussed in the article. How emotionally you write depends on the type of hook and the material itself. The various types of hooks are easily divided into four general groups. All four groups are adaptable to the factual article, but the fictional article confines itself to the last group.

DECLARATIVE GROUP

The declarative hooks factually state the general subject and promise further information. Most of this group are adaptations of newspaper leads.

1. *Summary*

The summary hook tells the reader *who* did *what, when,*

where, why, and sometimes *how.* It summarizes and emphasizes the value of the forthcoming development in the article. Your material generally designates whether to use all or any number of the W-words.

> Three months after I purchased a new car, the paint began to peel on the hood. I drove straight to the dealer who calmed me with the assurance I was covered by the guarantee.

2. *Capsule Sentence*

If you want to get immediately into the development of the article so you can give the reader the information he seeks, begin with the capsule sentence.

> Correct procedure gets good results from guarantees.

3. *Shocker*

The shocker or bullet sentence differs from the capsule in that it has more punch.

> Stop! Read that guarantee!

4. *Definition*

In English composition, you were taught to begin your essay with a definition of the subject. If the subject is unfamiliar, a definition is a good hook. With familiar subjects, you can create your own definition.

> A guarantee consists of an irritated buyer and a doubtful adjuster.

5. *Problem*

This hook declares that a problem, common to many readers, exists and promises that the article will offer a specific solution.

> Everyone at some time has asked a company to stand behind its guarantee. Not everyone has been completely satisfied with the results. Perhaps the fault was yours.

6. *Question*

The question is an inverted declarative statement. Because a spoken question seems to get quick attention, novice writers dogmatically hook every article with this device. While some of the better markets occasionally buy articles with a question hook, it appears predominantly in the lesser paying ones.

If you are determined to use the question hook, then let the question follow a factual statement or end the paragraph.

> *Wrong:* Did you check the guarantee when you bought a typewriter?

> *Right:* So you bought a new typewriter. Did you check the guarantee before you paid for it?

QUOTATION GROUP

Like the question, the quotation hook also strongly attracts the new writer. Unless you have a fresh approach, avoid it! With few exceptions, it has been greatly over-worked. Knowing the different types of quotation hooks will help you avoid the trite ones.

1. *Epigram*

An epigram is a short, witty saying. It offers good nostalgic value for reader identity if it is familiar.

> "Never put off until tomorrow" or your guarantee may expire.

2. *Parody*

For a parody, you change the meaning of a well-known or easily recognized quotation.

> I think that I shall never see, a paper so lovely as a guarantee. Especially is this true when a product proves defective.

3. *Literary Quotation*

The literary quotation takes a bit of poetry or prose and applies the selection to the general subject. Do not stretch or strain to make the quotation appropriate to the subject. Books of collected quotations or proverbs are a great help and inexpensive in paperback. Look for the key word of the subject in the index and find the most fitting quotation.

> One poet writes, "The little cares that fretted me, I lost them yesterday." You may share this feeling if you use your guarantee when a product proves defective.

4. *Statement of a Person*

The statement of a person, famous or little known, is short and emphasizes the subject of your article. An added bonus is to quote a person associated with the field of interest, but this is not essential. Always identify the person before you give the quotation. Whenever the remark comes from a copyrighted source, give the reference.

> Recently the president of Zippyzee Products Inc. stated, "The guarantee is only as good as the company which stands behind it."

5. *Statistics*

Even though figures are easily manipulated to lie, many people find them most convincing.

> According to a recent survey, four out of every ten people failed to use the guarantee when a product became defective.

JANUS GROUP

This group of hooks was named for the Roman god Janus who could see in two different directions at the same time. Devised by feature writers and syndicated columnists, these hooks also challenge the reader to look in two directions.

1. *Comparison or Contrast*

Compare or contrast a person, place, or fact pertinent to the subject matter in the article.

One hour your new wrist watch kept perfect time
and the next it stopped. Your thoughts, no doubt,
turned quickly to the guarantee.

2. *Historical Reference*

This hook compares a person, place, or event from the
past with the present.

At the turn of the century, to demand a written
guarantee on a purchased product was an insult to
the integrity of the neighbor or friend who sold it.
If the product didn't work, you returned it.

In the atomic age, the written warranty has replaced this personal contact between dealer and
purchaser. Unfortunately, the customer, no longer
armed with the weapon of friendship, is strictly at
the mercy of the dealer.

3. *Case History*

Case histories of people who have similar experiences
provide a good standard for the reader to judge his own
actions. If you select the cases from a wide geographical
area and from a variety of people, your problem appears
more important and widespread.

In California, a working mother arrived home late
to find the automatic oven cold and the meat un-
cooked.

A New York housewife opened the refrigerator
door and discovered the food frozen.

In Texas, a career woman started to vacuum the

living room rug when the machine whined to a halt.

Eventually, when these women can think rationally, they will remember the unexpired guarantee on the appliances.

4. *Reversal*

The reversal depends on anti-climax for effect. You lead the reader's thoughts in one direction and then do an about face. Comedians use this device in their monologues.

There I sat in my dream car with convertible top, bucket seats, and a dead battery. But the guarantee gave me back my dream.

FICTIONAL GROUP

To compete with fiction, the article writer has borrowed the short story hooks. Although these hooks emphasize emotion, they are not as dramatic as those of the short story.

1. *Action*

In the factual article, the action hook depicts a character on scene with a reader identity problem. The mood varies as: humorous, dramatic, nostalgic, or thought provoking.

One gray morning a California housewife filled her six months old dryer with a load of damp clothes, then set the dial. Nothing happened! She banged the door open and shut, pulled the plug and pushed it tighter into the outlet, and finally replaced the fuse. The dryer remained stubbornly silent. Once she began to think rationally, she remembered the guarantee.

The fictional article opens with action when the problem situation is of greater importance than the characterization. A personality sketch opens with the character in action any time a quick association with the individual's background or field of success is desired.

> Ed Harvey placed the metal frame on the wooden table beside the alphabetical sections of type. With unerring rapidity, he converted the galleys into front page make-up of *The Banner*. In a matter of hours, this four-page weekly, printed in a small Texas town, would begin its journey to Americans in China, Europe, South America, and other far-flung places.

2. *Character Trait*

The factual article opens with the character trait hook as a device to establish the authority of the author.

> I am overly conscious of performance. Each time I buy a new product, I carefully check the reputation of the company as well as the provisions of the guarantee. When a product develops a defect, I notify the proper authority immediately.

In the fictional article, if the character trait of the viewpoint or the major character creates the problem and the successive complications, you open with this hook.

> My wife has a southern drawl, and I am con-

stantly amazed at its curative powers. She literally
hypnotizes her victims and wins them to her way of
thinking before they recover consciousness.

The humor article will show how the wife wins her battles
with a drawl, even those with the husband who knows how
she works.

3. *Theme*

The factual article opens with the capsule sentence as
a hook and then proves the contention in the development.
The theme of the fictional article comes at the end as a sum-
mation of what the events proved. With this hook, the fictional writer borrows from the factual and gives the theme
before the events which prove it.

> Success to my father was proving that nothing
> was impossible. He referred to this as practicing the
> possible. In our small West Texas town, no one, not
> even Mother, took stock in his belief. She called it
> practicing the impossible and had developed an extra
> sensory perception which almost instantly detected
> Father's outlandish projects, such as the cyclone cellar.

Only a part of the total theme is stated in the hook. At
the end of the article Mother gives the complete theme:
"Practicing the possible to your father is an impossible
belief in the occurrence of the improbable."

4. *Setting*

Setting projects a very strong emotion; consequently it
is rarely used as a hook for the factual article. When the

background of a fictional article plays an important role in
the events of the piece, the setting hook is the best. This
example projects the trailer which plays a major role in the
events of the personal experience.

> That July afternoon the trailer was like an oven,
> but I was not aware of the heat. The man from Joe's
> construction company mopped his red face as he
> squeezed into one of the small trailer chairs.
> "You're more fortunate than most widows. Joe's
> accidental death gives you his full salary for three
> years." He fumbled with the clasp of his brief case.
> "If you want to sell this trailer—"
> "No—never!" This was our home and must keep on
> being our home. The trailer was the only way I knew
> of keeping Joe with me.

These are the basic hooks for the article. A versatile
writer creates new hooks by combining two or more basic
hooks to better project his material. Try it.

SUGGESTED PRACTICE

Practice writing an example of each type of hook illustrated in this chapter with the idea of using special ones
for your five article ideas.

5.

Keying
the Informative Article

The simplest and easiest article to write is the informative, which is a compilation of already established facts. Its concise presentation gives the reader an unbiased, thumbnail sketch of the subject.

The first step in writing this type of article is to develop the slant.

THE SLANT

The beginner immediately sits down to the typewriter and tries to expand his idea into a finished article. The professional writer proceeds more cautiously by working out a slant sheet. Arranging the ten variable factors of an article to coincide with the specifications of a given market is the *slant*. Each of the nine types of articles continuously in demand by editors of magazines has a basic slant.

The best approach to developing a slant sheet is to find the key word. The key word for the informative article is *information*.

1. *Market*

The market for the informative article includes: home service, women's magazines, religious, juvenile, business, science, travel, craft, sports, and outdoor. Usually the informative article appears as a one-column piece at the front or back of a magazine.

The present tendency of some editors is to group these articles in large encyclopedic sections or else in a special questions-answers format. In these special sections, the editor purchases the idea only and assigns a staff member to write it.

While each magazine has special requirements, the groups mentioned above share the same general slant. Little rewording is necessary to adapt an article to the special requirements; consequently your best opportunity for selling is to slant for the group rather than a single magazine.

To learn market requirements, study at least six issues of a magazine. If the magazine is one of a group, analyze six issues of two or more in a group. The final chapter gives more on market analysis.

2. *Subject*

The subject matter depends upon the type of magazine. The religious magazines, so called because they are published by church denominations, want informative articles dealing with problems in family living. Business publications buy information pertinent to their trade or profession. The younger juvenile magazines prefer articles on history, science, or geography. The older juveniles concentrate on personal problems such as make-up, popularity, or careers.

Home service magazines emphasize decoration, easier ways of doing difficult tasks around the house, refinishing furniture, or crafts of any kind. In the women's magazine, any subject which helps the housewife live better and save valuable time and energy will sell.

Informative travel articles appear in all types of magazines as well as specialties and business house organs. Any interesting trip or place is a likely subject. The popular craft and science market uses subjects dealing with mechanical devices, electronics, or photography.

Suggested subjects for informative articles are: discount houses, insurance, diet, medical care, investments, wedding etiquette, house plants, kinds of furniture, glassware, team teaching, teaching credentials, exchange students, types of furniture polish, wonder drugs, or postage rates.

3. *Length*

The length of the article is one of the most important factors in slanting. An amateur writes an article as long as he desires, but the professional does it to specification. Editors do not have time to cut wordage or expand it; so they are more likely to buy the article with the correct length. The informative article varies in length from 400 to 800 words, but check the magazine you wish to sell or special market information to get the exact wordage. The correct length convinces the editor that you have studied his magazine and know his needs.

An easy way to check the wordage in a printed article or on a typewritten sheet is to measure six inches and count the number of words in each. Figure out the average number of words to an inch. To find the total wordage, multiply the average number of words by the entire measurement.

To simplify this further, figure out how many words you get to an average typewritten page and merely multiply the number by the total pages. This average ranges from 250 to 300 words per page, depending on the margins you set on the typewriter. In giving the word count, state it in the nearest hundred as 1500—not 1534 words.

4. *Viewpoint*

Since you report established facts and do not insert your personal opinion, the viewpoint is objective. You write: "One must be careful in applying the paint" and not "You must be careful in applying the paint." This impersonal, objective reporting appears more convincing to the reader.

There are always exceptions. Those markets which buy the idea and staff-write the article frequently substitute the impersonal *you* for *one*. Since contributors of fillers naturally write in first person, the personal *you* and the intimate *I* are gradually appearing in the informative article. To make your choice, study the magazine you wish to sell and follow its specification.

5. *Reader Reaction*

When you write an article, you decide what reaction you wish from your reader. In the informative article, the reaction of the reader is practically predetermined. He seeks information on a subject, and you provide it in an objective, concise, and easily remembered manner. If you write your directions so understandably that he will have no difficulty following them, you have achieved the correct reader reaction for the informative article.

6. *Immediacy*

Immediacy is a deadline in time after which the information is no longer of value to the reader. There is no immediacy to an informative article. These already established facts are as timely today as they will be tomorrow or ten years from now. As in encyclopedias, new developments are added periodically. Directions for using a library have not changed in years. So the reader seeks information he may utilize now or at some indefinite date.

7. *Red String*

The facts presented in your article are tied together with a dominant thought called a *red string*. Professionals know the red string as a *transition* which provides unity for the article. Transitions are discussed in Chapter 17.

In the informative article, the capsule sentence is the red string. You repeat a key word or a synonym with each new point you discuss. Sometimes the editor will take the capsule sentence of your article and let it serve as the title. In this event, the title becomes the single story thread of your article.

8. *Title*

A good title catches the attention of the editor and the reader. Most professional writers rely on a working title to keep them on the subject, as the capsule sentence or a key phrase.

When you complete the article, generally some phrase you have used in it will catch your eye and give you a most provocative title. Look through the magazines you wish to sell and study the titles. How many words do they contain? Are they clever or do they merely state the subject? When you have analyzed a large number of titles, create a similar one for your piece.

9. *Author's Image*

Since the reader's interest in this type of article is for information, he wants correct facts. You must carefully research the information from all sources, then you condense and simplify the facts for the reader in an unbiased presentation. The author-image is that of a careful researcher and unbiased thinker.

10. *Style*

Most readers want information brief, simple, and understandable; therefore you write the information in short, factual sentences with strong transitions between paragraphs. A good arrangement is a step-by-step approach, numbering if possible, in a chronological or logical organization.

Slant Sheet on Guarantees

To be sure that you follow the market requirements, work out an informative slant sheet for your general idea. Here is one on the guarantee idea.

1. *Market:* digest, home service, women's magazines
2. *Subject:* guarantees
3. *Length:* 800 words
4. *Viewpoint:* objective
5. *Reader Reaction:* to get information
6. *Immediacy:* none
7. *Red String:* capsule sentence and key word—guarantee and warranty
8. *Title:* All About Guarantees
9. *Author's Image:* careful researcher and unbiased thinker
10. *Style:* simple and concise

When a professional completes his slant sheet, he then turns his attention to the article pattern.

The Pattern

Through the years professional writers have developed certain basic patterns which transpose an idea into an article. A *pattern* is an adaptation of the general formula to the material and the slant. The adaptation may take three forms: 1. follow the formula exactly, 2. emphasize specific parts more than others, or 3. apply only certain sections.

Developing an individual pattern from a general formula is one of the creative processes of professional writing. The truly informative article finds only three parts of the formula essential.

1. *Hook*

Since the reader is looking for this special information, he actually hooks himself when he turns to any section of a magazine featuring this type of article. As a result, no hook is required.

While some editors are deviating from the no-hook format, they do restrict the opening to one or two brief sentences. If the market you choose puts a hook on an informative article, it is probably a definition, problem, question, or statistic. Select the hook which best showcases your material.

2. *Capsule Sentence*

Most informative articles begin with a capsule sentence; consequently you need a strong statement which will provide at least three good points for development and which will also hook the reader's attention. At the same time, the sentence is brief and to the point.

3. *Authority*

The location in the magazine or the type of journal implies your authority along with the actual presentation of facts. The way you develop your facts shows whether you did surface or depth research.

4. *Development*

The simplest way to develop the facts is to follow the newspaper formula of *who, when, where, why,* and *what.* Your material will indicate whether you need all or only part of these W-words.

When you know the points you wish to develop, you are ready to do research. Most research begins with a check of the *Reader's Guide* at the library and a study of previously published articles on the subject. In addition to published sources, you will do some primary research, such as interviewing people associated with the field.

The final step in your research is to correlate the most important facts and answer the questions listed in your development. Do not quote directly from specific individuals without their written permission. Your misquote can result in a suit. The safest approach is to mention no names but give your personal analysis and deductions from your research.

5. *Conclusion*

Most informative articles arrange the points for development so that the last one connects strongly with the capsule sentence. When this is done, no conclusion is necessary. In the event that the points for develpment are numbered, also omit the conclusion.

When the points for development are rather weak or the numbers have several subheads, a short conclusion strengthens and pinpoints the essentials for the reader. Again, let your material guide you.

6. *Twist*

Omit the twist. Since the reader came to you, he leaves when he secures his information. Cleverness at the end often results in loss of confidence or mistrust, so state your facts and exit quickly.

Although this pattern appears simple, applying it to your general idea is the only way of making sure you know how to do this article.

Work Sheet on Guarantees

Most professional writers use a work sheet to organize their thoughts and to follow when making the first draft on the article. To do a work sheet, you write the hook, capsule sentence, conclusion, and twist exactly as they appear in your article. The development states each point in a brief sentence or question. As you become more experienced in writing, you will learn to organize some of this information in your head.

Since the pattern for the informative article does not include the hook, conclusion, and twist, the work sheet actually contains only the capsule sentence and the points to develop. Here is a work sheet on the guarantee idea.

1. *Hook:* none
2. *Capsule Sentence:* Everyone should learn about guarantees.
3. *Authority:* implied in the section of the magazine,

the type of magazine, but mostly through the presentation of facts

4. *Points to Develop:*
   What is a guarantee?
   Where is it given?
   Who gives it?
   When is it used?
   Why is it valuable?

5. *Conclusion:* none

6. *Twist:* none

Suggested Practice

Make a slant and a work sheet for an informative article from your general idea.

6.

The How-to-do-it
Article

The how-to-do-it article emphasizes clearness of directions and success in a previously tested accomplishment. Unlike the informative, the how-to uses subjective viewpoint and a dominant emotion.

The Slant

The slant of the informative article is a re-hash of known facts on a general subject, but the how-to deals with action done originally by you. So the key word is *do*.

1. *Market*

Almost every magazine buys some variety of the how-to article. Digest, home service, science, craft, business, travel, and juvenile magazines publish several in each issue. In recent years, much of the how-to in women's magazines and home service has become staff written, narrowing the chances for a sale by a free-lance writer.

2. *Subject*

The subject covers any tested process which instructs the reader in a specific accomplishment. The important criterion is that it is of interest to enough readers so you have a wide choice of markets. Even if your subject attracts only a few readers, a specialty magazine may buy it. Finding that specialty magazine is the problem.

The how-to article covers such specific subjects as meeting new clients, making a speech, sewing a coat, barbecuing a turkey, making furniture, decorating a child's room, getting a job, taking pictures—the list is endless. In fact, any action explicable in five to ten easy steps is a subject for a how-to article.

3. *Length*

The how-to article runs from 800 to 1500 words, rarely longer. Check the writer's market information for the exact length in the magazine you wish to sell, or determine the wordage by reading six issues of the magazine. If you cannot cover your subject in the required length, either you do not know the important facts of your subject or this is not material for a how-to article.

4. *Viewpoint*

The how-to article offers a choice of two types of subjective viewpoint. The easiest and the most popular is the *you* or imperative mood, as in: "Set a deadline for action." The directions given imply the *I* of the author. The other type of viewpoint opens with I-the-author, relating a short experience, then shifts quickly to you-the-reader for the directions. At the conclusion, you circle back to I-the-author.

5. *Reader Reaction*

From the first word you want the reader to feel *confident* that he can accomplish what you have done successfully. You consistently assure the reader that the task is simple if he follows these directions and that failure is practically impossible. To strengthen the confidence further, anticipate possible problems or protests from the reader and show him that the fears are groundless.

6. *Immediacy*

Not only do you assure the reader he can do it but you urge him to act now; consequently the immediacy is strong. You cannot urge the reader too strongly to get his supplies and go to work. Warn him against putting off until tomorrow.

7. *Red String*

While the capsule sentence is the primary red string, you need secondary support. The reader for the how-to article is not necessarily seeking your material as in the informative, so you need a tightly written piece to catch and hold his interest until he believes he can accomplish the task.

The spirit of confidence gives this secondary unity. Each step of the development must imply confidence. The listing of materials and numbering of steps add to this continuity as does the strong *you* viewpoint. Omit any doubtful or negative statements. This assumption of ability breeds confidence, as does the simplicity of the instructions.

8. *Title*

The working title is long and includes the key words *how to do,* such as "How to Get Better Results on Guarantees." The how-to in the working title emphasizes the instructional tone in your mind and keeps you on the single story thread. When you finish, select an action title with verbs such as: "Get Results on Guarantees."

9. *Author's Image*

The market and the material shape the image. Material dealing with building a piece of furniture designates the author as a man who knows construction and a market such as home service or crafts.

As long as the material comes from your own experience, you have no difficulty projecting the author-image to the reader. The difficulty comes when you take another person's experience and step into his identity. To help you assume his identity, write a character sketch in the first person telling what experience he has had, how he works, what he likes. Then your directions will carry a stronger conviction.

10. *Style*

Wordiness collects rejection slips for this type of article
since brevity breeds confidence when giving instructions.
Likewise, the reader wants to get the step-by-step process
as quickly and easily as possible so that he can do it himself. He will not waste time wading through your beautiful
adjectives or "cute" phrases to dig out the instructions.

Merely list the necessary materials, number the essential
steps, and draw sketches to blueprint the process explained.
If you cannot diagram, photographs are equally explicit.

SLANT SHEET ON GUARANTEES

   cations

2. *Subject:* how to use a guarantee

1. *Market:* home service, digest, business publi-
3. *Length:* 1000 words

4. *Viewpoint:* I-you combination

5. *Reader Reaction:* confidence to act

6. *Immediacy:* now

7. *Red String:* capsule sentence, emotion of confidence, and step-by-step presentation

8. *Title:* Get Results on Guarantees

9. *Author's Image:* a housewife who has been reasonably successful in getting action on guarantees

10. *Style:* simple and brief, blueprinting the action

THE PATTERN

The pattern of the how-to article follows that of the formula exactly. As a result, this type of article is not only easy to write but also is a quick sale for the novice.

1. *Hook*

The best hooks for the *I-you* viewpoint are: action, problem, or character trait. You show how the *I* put off doing a task because he lacked confidence, then did it successfully. Shift to the *you* and tell the reader not to procrastinate because the task is only a matter of easy steps.

The *you* viewpoint adapts easily to these hooks: summary, question, capsule sentence, problem, definition, comparison, or contrast.

A combination of two or more hooks often does an even better job of catching the reader's attention. The hook, however, must fit the material.

2. *Capsule Sentence*

The capsule sentence clearly states what the reader can accomplish if he follows the instructions given in the article.

3. *Authority*

The device to establish your authority varies with markets. Any of these are used: implied in the market or in the location in a special section; placed in the by-line or footnote; stated in a sentence or shown in the instructive way you present the facts.

4. Development

When you do a physical task, such as redecorating a room or building a bookcase, you list the physical equipment needed and the approximate cost. This is quite detailed, giving the exact number of boards, the length of each, the nails, glue, tools. List every item no matter how small. Some authors even estimate the approximate number of hours required to complete the task.

Once you have listed the materials, you number each step of action to provide a word blueprint. If you can draw, sketches or diagrams make the material more salable. In the event the task is rather difficult and you do not have sketches, the magazine will provide them.

Many how-to articles use eight by ten glossy black and white photographs to illustrate the steps listed in the copy. Write the cutlines or captions on typing paper and glue them to the bottom of the picture so that the editor may read while he looks. This typed information is folded up so that the photographs fit into the envelope for mailing.

Any information put in the captions does not appear in the article. In some instances, the how-to article consists only of instructional pictures. When decorating or modernizing a room or home, always take before and after pictures. If you are building a project, take step-by-step pictures.

The how-to article does not always deal with a construction project; pieces which give instructions on how to write a letter, how to set up a filing system, or how to cut out a dress are included also in this pattern. These subjects pertain likewise to action.

5. *Conclusion*

Briefly urge the reader to get to work and assure him of success. If you can do it, you tell him, so can he.

6. *Twist*

The twist usually emphasizes the personal accomplishment of the reader.

Work Sheet on Guarantees

1. *Hook:* Everyone at some time has asked a company to stand behind its guarantee. Not everyone has been completely satisfied with the results. Perhaps the fault is yours.
2. *Capsule Sentence:* Correct procedure gets results.
3. *Authority:* In the past ten years I have used guarantees with good results on items that vary from watches to cars.
4. *Development:*
   Know the limits of your guarantee.
   At first sign of defect, notify the proper authority by letter, telephone, or in person.
   Set a reasonable deadline for results.
   If no action, write the president of the company briefly summarizing the case.

5. *Conclusion:* The next time a product develops a defect, put this procedure into action.

6. *Twist:* The results will please you.

Suggested Practice

Develop a slant and work sheet for a how-to-do-it article from your general idea.

7.

Illustrative Examples
When and *How* to Use Them

Most articles rely on *fictional* devices to project a word picture of the factual statement to the reader. You state the point for development and then show the meaning with an example. Once you learn the five basic devices for illustrating an article, you can devise combinations especially tailored for your material.

QUOTATIONS

Your library, the chamber of commerce, public relation departments of large companies, and many other sources offer unlimited quotable material. The subject of your article determines the best of these sources.

1. *Statistics*

Figures look very convincing in black and white; hence, you select those figures which will support and prove the capsule sentence and the points developed in your article. You may either quote the statistic and draw the conclusion for the reader or make a factual statement and prove it with statistics.

Be sure your statistics reinforce, prove, or dramatize your factual statement. In this example the figures are presented as a startling fact and applied to the problem of acting on a guarantee.

> Statistics show that only one out of ten people will take action to remedy a situation which has a simple solution with a guarantee. Yet a large majority are quick to complain to everyone but the authority who issued the guarantee. Unless the buyer uses his guarantee, there is nothing the company can do.

When only the basic statistics are available, you do the computing yourself. The quickest way to lose a reader, however, is to draw exaggerated conclusions which obviously make statistics lie. Always make your statistical deductions logical and plausible.

2. *People*

Quotations from important and well-known people impress readers. You state your point, then show that the experts associated with the subject agree with you. Quote accurately! Frequently, a clearance from the person quoted is necessary. If you quote a printed source, give credit in a footnote.

> T. Grover Harris, in charge of customer's service for the Kemp Department Stores, quoted a special survey as showing that nine out of ten customers prefer to take care of a small adjustment at their own expense rather than comply with the red tape of a guarantee.

3. *Published References*

Published references which are copyrighted include books, encyclopedias, magazine articles, and some bulletins or pamphlets. Taking a short quotation from this material needs no clearance as long as you give the source. When you quote from these sources, summarize the material preceding the quotation so as to avoid taking it completely out of context. Random quotations independent of context convey a different meaning from the original intent.

> James Henry West states in his "History of Merchandising" that the guarantee was first used in the nineteenth century to sell medicine. The seller offered to refund the money if the medicine did not cure the ten ailments listed. There is no record of how many refunds were made.

Whether you quote statistics, people, or texts, check yourself carefully for accuracy and acknowledge the source.

RAPID NARRATION

Possibly the most natural way to illustrate a fact is by narration, a device you learned in writing English compositions. Narration is dull unless you give it urgency with a problem, a conflict, and a solution.

> Three months after I purchased a new car, the paint cracked. I complained to the dealer who promised to contact the district office. A month passed and nothing happened. I wrote the district office. Another month passed. I wrote the president of the company at the home office. In three days, an adjuster contacted me and authorized a paint job.

Although action verbs and short sentences are used to speed the flow of words, you may confuse this with another device called emotional reminiscence.

EMOTIONAL REMINISCENCE

Any time you compare the present-day situation with what existed in the past, you illustrate the point with emotional reminiscence. You lead into the illustration with such transitional phrases as: "when I was growing into manhood," "as a child, I remember," or "I recall during the Roaring Twenties."

> Looking back into my childhood, I recall that Mother and Grandmother agreed on every subject except one—guarantees. When Grandmother decided to buy me a bike, Mother insisted on going along.

As soon as I selected the bike, Mother asked about the guarantee.

Grandmother looked pained and reminded that she was buying the bike. Mother pointed out that she would be the one to keep it working. This was the signal for Grandmother to give her sermon on how she selected a dealer with integrity and didn't have to rely on a worthless slip of paper. She paid for the bike with a roll of bills from her enormous purse, then took me by the hand and led me from the store.

Mother stayed behind, obviously to get the guarantee. As it turned out, the guarantee was the only way Mother did force the dealer to replace the defective parts at no cost.

This device is written in long rambling sentences to show the action and the conflict. While it is more emotional than narration, it does not have the punch of dramatic action.

DRAMATIC ACTION

Dramatic action takes the reader on scene to encounter the problem and share the action leading to a solution. Short punchy sentences, action verbs, and rapid rhythm of words project the dramatic quality.

My husband did the unexpected. He remembered my birthday with red roses. An hour after I put them in water, they wilted. I stuck them in ice water, but they did not revive. I crumbled an aspirin in the

water. They looked sicker. I stuck them in the refrigerator.

Finally, I snatched up the telephone to dial the
number of the florist, then I banged the receiver in
the cradle. This demanded a written protest so the
florist could put it in his files for future reference.
I tossed the first version into the wastebasket and
dashed off a less heated one.

The next day I received fresh red roses and printed
information on how to revive wilted cut flowers.

This device compresses the conflicts of a scene to action
alone. While this example shows the actions of only one
person, another might show those of two or more people in
conflict.

SERIES OF INCIDENTS

An *incident* is any action where two or more characters
are not in conflict. A series of incidents does imply conflict
if they are arranged in hindrances and furtherances. When
a person acts but fails to solve the problem, it is a *hindrance*.
When he tries and has some success or does succeed, the
result is a *furtherance*. Your material suggests the number
and the arrangement of hindrance-furtherance incidents.

When I bought a portable washer from a large
department store, the guarantee covered ninety days.
The motor stopped sixty days later. I wrote the small
appliance department of the store.

Back came a reply by return mail stating that the

store no longer carried this appliance and therefore could not stand behind the guarantee. I wrote customer's service which sent an address and suggested I contact the factory.

I wrote the president of the store, briefly summarizing my efforts to get service. I concluded by saying I was surprised that his store did not live up to its fine reputation.

In addition to a letter of apology, I received a new washer of a different brand but comparable to the defective one.

In this example, the quick reply is a furtherance while the refusal is a hindrance. The name of the factory is a furtherance, but no restitution is a hindrance. The receipt of the washer and apology is a conclusive furtherance. This hindrance-furtherance arrangement of incidents ranks second in fictional quality only to the scene.

THE SCENE

The most fictional illustration is a scene which depicts conflict between two or more people. Because the scene in the factual article is more compact than in a short story, you build the structure around the W-words. In a sentence or a short paragraph, you summarize the problem situation by telling *when, where,* and *who.*

I complained three times and waited six months for the department store to replace the defective shelf on my refrigerator door. Then I went personally to the manager's office.

The *what* tersely develops the conflict through action and dialogue between the individuals involved.

> "Incredible," the manager exclaimed when I related my story and he immediately telephoned customer's service to verify. He hung up chagrined. "I'll have a repair man at your home within the hour."

Summarize the outcome.

> The repairman arrived thirty minutes later and installed a new shelf.

The scene in the fictional article, explained in Chapter 13, approximates that of the short story.

Emotional reminiscence, dramatic action, and a series of incidents are often substituted for scenes in both the short story and the fictional article to speed the pace and to meet the market requirement on length. Most of these illustrating devices become stronger dramatically and more effective emotionally when combined with another.

Always place each illustration on a separate sheet of paper as you did the points for discussion. Then you can easily slip these sheets between your points for discussion.

SUGGESTED PRACTICE

Based on your general idea, write an illustration of each device so that you can incorporate them later in the next two types of articles.

8.

Building
the Idea Article

The idea article deals with a mental adjustment to an existing problem in everyday living. While the how-to emphasizes the solution to a recognized problem, the idea article must first prove the existence of a problem before it suggests a logical solution. Through this problem-solution procedure, you-the-author actually do the thinking for the reader. You help him diagnose his problem and provide the sensible solution.

THE SLANT

The key word for this slant is *practical*.

1. *Market*

All magazines buy some form of the idea article, making

it one of the best sellers. The only limitation on market is the subject.

2. *Subject*

Any article which discusses problems in living, such as buying a house or a car, has a wide reader appeal and an unlimited market. On the other hand, problems in school administration narrow the reader interest to school administrators and a professional journal market.

Subjects must touch the daily living of people: retirement, travel, religion, budgets, career, family, education, death, crime, or food.

3. *Length*

This article varies in length from 1800 words to 3000, with 2000 the most acceptable. Check the magazine you wish to sell for the preferred length.

4. *Viewpoint*

Before you choose the viewpoint, decide whether the article will include your experiences exclusively or a combination of yours and several other people's. For your experiences alone, the first person viewpoint is imperative. Either the implied or the *I-you* combination is more effective with mixed experiences.

5. *Reader Reaction*

The idea article appeals to the reader's logic and common sense. You urge him to think intelligently about his problem and work out a sensible solution. The key to this practical emotion is to select a strong reader identity problem.

6. *Immediacy*

This article has a dual immediacy: now or in the near future. If the reader shares the problem, he will benefit now. Otherwise, he will need the information when he has such a problem. Since this is not necessarily deadline material, the facts in the article may prevent the problem from arising in the reader's life at a future date.

7. *Red String*

The capsule sentence joins with the problem-solution development and the sensible emotion to provide the unity. On occasion, an object, a person, or a place link the examples. More transitional devices are needed for continuity as wordage increases.

8. *Title*

The title relates either to the reader identity problem or the practical solution. Avoid cleverness but do incorporate a challenge. The working title is a shortened form of the capsule sentence.

9. *Author's Image*

The author is a sensible individual who can analyze a problem and find a logical and practical solution.

10. *Style*

With this pattern, you desert the simple style and resort

to more compound and complex sentences. Strong action verbs and descriptive phrases are popular. Although the examples which illustrate your points rely on such fictional techniques as tags, dialogue, and other emotional projection devices, the arrangement of the points stresses the practical and earthy approach.

SLANT SHEET ON GUARANTEES

1. *Market:* digest, home service, religious
2. *Subject:* Be practical and use your guarantee
3. *Length:* 2000 words
4. *Viewpoint:* first person
5. *Reader Reaction:* to think with common sense
6. *Immediacy:* act today or tomorrow
7. *Red String:* capsule sentence, problem-solution arrangement, common-sense emotion
8. *Title:* Benefit from Guarantees
9. *Author's Image:* a practical housewife who uses her guarantees
10. *Style:* logical but dramatic

THE PATTERN

Although the idea pattern contains all parts of the formula, its individuality comes from the presentation of the problem-solution development and the source of the material. Three different sources are available: your own personal experiences exclusively, the experiences of a number of other people, or a combination of yours and others'.

1. *Hook*

The hook, strong and challenging, stresses the reader identity problem. Since the article runs around 2000 words, the hook is longer proportionately. In restricting the article to your experiences alone, choose any of the fictional hooks.

The most appropriate hooks for the experiences of others are: summary, comparison and contrast, case history, action, or problem. A combination of two or more types of hook makes a stronger opening and shows your creativeness. Historical reference blends well with comparison and contrast.

As a final check, read nothing but the hooks of articles in several issues of the magazine you wish to sell. What types appear most often? Can you improve on these?

2. *Capsule Sentence*

The capsule sentence is short and sensible, sometimes carrying a slightly shocking note to get immediate attention. At the same time, this sentence must clearly state your reaction to the reader identity problem demanding a solution.

3. *Authority*

In a paragraph or two, tell the reader how extensively you have researched your subject—the where, when, why, and how of your investigation. Let the illustrations further assure the reader of your authority. This combination of devices will convince the reader that you can solve the problem with common sense.

4. *Development*

The development helps the reader analyze the problem and then outlines the practical solution. The idea pattern offers a choice of two types of development with the selection dependent upon the reader identity problem.

The specific reader identity problem based upon your experiences alone usually follows this organization. One-half of the development presents the problem and shows how it grew worse. The remainder pictures the steps leading to the solution. Here is the general organization.

1. *The Problem*
   a. First occurrence of problem
   b. New complications
   c. Crisis demanding action

2. *The Solution*
   a. First step
   b. Second step
   c. Final solution

The strong continuity of working from one problem to one solution by a single individual requires fictional treatment similar to that of the short story because each illustration leads to the next and further complicates the situation. You build to a dramatic crisis and then logically descend back to earth.

The second type of development emphasizes a general reader identity problem which has happened to you or a group of people. The reader finds assistance or prevents such a problem from occurring by reading the article. All the illustrations relate to the general problem but not necessarily to each other.

For this development, you divide the problem into a series of small ones, using your W-words, and show how you solved each with common sense. By solving the lesser problems, you automatically provide the solution to the larger one.

To utilize the information in the idea article, the reader must believe it. You state a fact and illustrate with examples the reader may have experienced himself. This factual structure maintains the veracity, and the illustrations establish the reader identity through plausibility.

5. *Conclusion*

The multi-experience conclusion urges the reader to apply this information at the first opportunity, promising him personal betterment through this sensible approach to everyday problems. The single experience concludes with a longer statement of what you learned and transfers this learning to the reader for future use.

6. *Twist*

The twist always relates to the hook and urges the reader to act sensibly now or in the near future.

WORK SHEET ON GUARANTEES

1. *Hook:* I am overly conscious of performance. Each time I buy a new product, I carefully check the reputation of the company as well as the provi-

sions of the guarantee. When a product develops a defect, I notify the proper authority immediately.

2. *Capsule Sentence:* Experience has taught me the value of a guarantee.

3. *Authority:* In the past ten years I have used guarantees with good results on items that vary from watches to cars.

4. *Development (series of problems):*

Guarantees make you more conscious of performance in a product.

roses—scene
draperies—dramatic action
typewriter—narration

Guarantees save money.

refrigerator shelf—series of incidents
gasket on washing machine—narration
floors—scene

Guarantees assist you with future purchases.

car—narration
raincoat—dramatic action
watch—series of incidents

Guarantees keep you a satisfied customer.

portable washing machine—narration
battery—series of incidents
tires—scene

Guarantees lead to unexpected replacements.

plastic bridge cards—incident
boy's watch—incident

5. *Conclusion:* The next time you have trouble with a product, be practical and contact the proper authority who issued the guarantee.

6. *Twist:* You have everything to gain.

Some of the examples cited are totally successful while others are partial replacements or failures. Too much success is not believable.

SUGGESTED PRACTICE

Adapt your general idea to this pattern, doing a slant and a work sheet. Note that this work sheet also lists the illustrations and the devices.

9.

The Controversial Article

The controversial article, as the name indicates, discusses issues with two sharply defined opinions. Although you present only one side of the argument, as in a debate, you carefully research both sides so you can anticipate and answer any argument from your opponents. This type of article commands very high pay because of the extensive research required and the explosiveness of the subject.

THE SLANT

This is the most biased of all the factual articles. While you present true facts, you select and arrange them in such a manner as to persuade the reader to accept your arguments as correct.

1. *Market*

The controversial nature of the article demands the polished technique of a professional who can deliver the bias without lawsuits against the magazine. The editor heistates to take a chance on the research of a newcomer; therefore most of these articles are written on assignment.

This does not mean that a beginner can not sell this type of article. You may be the exception if you are a careful researcher and can produce legal proof of your statements. If you are a newcomer to the field, many editors will pay an expert to check your facts. Since this is expensive, the trend is to buy from an established professional writer who has already proved himself a good researcher.

The best way to win recognition is to sell to the lesser markets and work your way up to the better ones. Double-check your research, or else one slip and you are out. At the top, you fight with the other professionals for the choice assignments.

The top markets for this article are the men's magazines, general magazines, literary, political, and business publications, or digest markets. Since the trend is toward specialization of interest, general magazines for both men and women are fast disappearing.

2. *Subject*

Almost any subject has a controversial angle, but some are stronger than others. The conflicts of the times are your indicators. Education is always a controversial matter. The three R's challenge the progressive plan of education. Team teaching is opposed to one teacher.

Most political subjects have two sides. Should justices of the peace be salaried or earn their pay through fines? Should civil service employees be given tenure? Should literacy be a requirement of voting? Should the government permit unlimited immigration? Should churches be taxed?

Problems of senior citizens provide several controversial issues involving medical care, retirement pay, or housing. The more explosive subject is better for a controversial bias.

3. *Length*

This article varies in length between 2000 and 5000 words. You need this many words to thoroughly convince your reader to think as you do. The digest market takes the shorter length.

4. *Viewpoint*

The implied viewpoint is best. Sometimes the author begins with an *I* if he is a member of a board or on the staff which represents one view. In the development of the article, the *I* recedes into the background as much as possible. Too much *I* makes the reader doubtful or suspicious of self-interest. With the implied viewpoint, you stay behind the scene but direct the emotional thinking with the facts and illustrations.

5. *Reader Reaction*

The reader reaction is always the same: a shocking miscarriage of justice which demands remedial action. Presenting the shocking facts in a convincing style earns a higher rate of pay. Raw shock goes to the cheaper and more sensa-tional markets.

6. *Immediacy*

The immediacy is strong. You urge the reader to act today to correct this miscarriage of justice.

7. *Red String*

Your chief transition is the capsule sentence stating your contention. Along with the dominant emotion of logic or reason, the research reinforces the red string.

8. *Title*

The working title is the capsule sentence. The article title is rather long and shocking, immediately throwing out a challenge to the reader.

9. *Author's Image*

The author must project a thinking man who is not easily swayed but who relies upon careful research to shape his opinions. As a reasonable and logical thinker, you walk an intellectual tightrope. One emotional misstep will lose your reader.

10. *Style*

You alternate between long and short sentences, giving the writing an up and down emotional impact. Above all, you must appear fair with the opponent. A good device is to assume that the reader has been fooled and admit that you-the-author were also blind to the facts until you did some careful research. Likewise, you agree that the opponent has a point, but you meet it with such a strong contention that you obliterate it. Keep reminding the reader that you want only to share this awakening within him so that he, too, can see the picture correctly.

SLANT SHEET ON GUARANTEES

1. *Market:* digest
2. *Subject:* Many dealers find ways to evade the guarantees they give
3. *Length:* 2000 words
4. *Viewpoint:* implied
5. *Reader Reaction:* Force dealers to stand behind guarantees
6. *Immediacy:* Act now
7. *Red String:* capsule sentence, researched authority, logical emotion
8. *Title:* Stop the Guarantee Racket
9. *Author's Image:* a thinking person who does his own investigating
10. *Style:* conciliatory on the surface but volcanic underneath

THE PATTERN

The controversial article uses all parts of the formula but in different proportions from those previously discussed. Key words for the pattern are *shock, reason,* and *reform.*

1. *Hook*

The hook, like those of the other articles, gets proportionately longer. If you write a total of 5000 words, the hook will cover approximately a page or 250 words. The hook for other lengths will follow this same proportion, as, for example, one-half page for 2500 words.

Viewpoint and hook are closely related. If you write from the viewpoint of a person associated first hand with the controversial subject, show yourself working on the job. With an implied viewpoint, take the reader on scene to experience what happens. Put the reader in touch immediately with the shocking situation and miscarriage of justice.

The choice of hooks includes: summary, problem, statement of a person, case history, shocker, contrast or comparison, action, and statistical. Good combinations are: action and statement of a person; problem and case history; statistical and shocker.

2. *Capsule Sentence*

The summary sentence pinpoints which side of the issue you plan to take. Make the sentence short and shocking so it shakes the reader into awareness of the injustice. A slow build-up with several long, rambling sentences preceding the shocker is most effective.

3. *Authority*

The authority is equal in length to the hook plus the capsule sentence paragraph. No reader will believe your challenging statements unless you show him *when, where, why,* and *how* you carried on your scholarly investigation. Explain the *how* of the research in most minute and scientific detail. Haphazard research alienates the reader before you even begin the argument. Impress the reader by unbiased research methods.

4. *Development*

With the reader's defenses low, the development presents biased but very reasonable proof of the shocking situation revealed in the hook, capsule sentence, and authority. Each argument, statement-by-statement, adds to the credibility of your picture. The W-words themselves provide an outline for the presentation of the material.

Logically presented facts, along with the potent and carefully assembled illustrations, sway the reader to accept your reactions. Compare these arguments with the weak and obviously biased ones of the opponent. Biased facts are covered with plausibility and reader identity situations. Exaggeration leads to doubt; hence you limit the bias to believable, everyday situations.

A weak argument frequently becomes more persuasive with two or three strong illustrations. A strong point is more convincing with a weak illustration since this implies there is no doubt as to the correctness of the statement. A dramatic illustration encourages the reader to think irrationally with his emotion rather than his head. Although you constantly remind the reader to think reasonably, you actually are thinking emotionally for him.

5. *Conclusion*

The conclusion strongly urges the reader to take immediate action and reform the present situation, but he cannot act until you present a feasible plan. Do not criticize unless you can present a better way of handling the situation; therefore blueprint the action you want him to take. Many controversial articles are rejected because they fail to present a plan for positive action.

The length of the conclusion varies with your plan for action. If the subject deals with a problem which most readers have been aware of for some time and numerous plans have been recommended, the development is a little shorter than the conclusion. You need more wordage to show why yours is the only workable plan.

Any time the reader is unaware of the situation under criticism, your development discusses in detail the necessity for reform. Winning the reader to your way of thinking is more important than the general plan you will propose; consequently the conclusion is equal in length to the combined wordage of the hook and capsule sentence.

When the reader is only vaguely aware of the injustice and several attempts have been made to remedy the situation, the conclusion is equal in length to the development. This is the most commonly used proportion.

6. *Twist*

The twist leaves the reader with thought-provoking words which place the responsibility of reform in his hands. An adaptation of a famous quotation is one way of challenging the reader to act now. Another device is to show the situation after reform, the reverse picture of the hook.

Work Sheet on Guarantees

1. *Hook:* At the turn of the century, to demand a written guarantee on a purchased product was an insult to the integrity of the neighbor or friend who sold it. If the product didn't work, you returned it.

   In the atomic age, the written warranty has replaced this personal contact between dealer and purchaser. Unfortunately, the customer, no longer armed with the weapon of friendship, is strictly at the mercy of the dealer.

2. *Capsule Sentence:* A guarantee is only as reliable as the company that gives it. A large number are worth less than the paper on which they are written because many dealers look upon a guarantee as a challenge to contrive escape hatches from legal responsibility.

3. *Authority:* A market research company devised a questionnaire and interviewed a representative sampling of people in regard to their experiences with companies and guarantees.

   The research company then analyzed the ballots and reported these startling results.

4. *Development:*

   50% of those interviewed found that dealers placed the blame on normal wear and tear.

   brass lamps—narration

automatic shift on car—series of incidents
shelf on refrigerator—scene

35% thought dealers escaped behind technicalities.

tires—dramatic action
watch—series of incidents

75% felt dealers resorted to the referral system.

portable washer—series of incidents
dryer—narration
floors—scene

40% said dealers made only partial adjustment.

typewriter—dramatic action
blanket—narration
raw silk fabric—scene

15% believed dealers demanded proof that could not be given under the conditions listed.

lawn mower—narration
television set—series of incidents

5. *Conclusion:* The only hope of remedying this situation is for all customers to follow the same plan. The minute a defect develops in any product, no matter how inconsequential, immediately give written or personal notice to the proper authority. Set a deadline for a reply.

When the date is reached and no effort has been made to remedy the situation, go in person again to the dealer and demand action. In the event that he does not have the authority to act, find out who does.

Contact this person and again set a date for a reply. If there is no answer, contact the president of the company by mail or in person. As a final resort, file suit in a small claims court.

6. *Twist:* If every individual demanded that dealers stand behind the products they guarantee, the warranty would become a very valuable document. So do your part and act today. Tomorrow is too late.

SUGGESTED PRACTICE

Write a slant and a work sheet for a controversial article from your general idea.

10.

The Inspirational Article

The inspirational article is a psychological how-to-do-it. The structure coincides with the factual formula, but the illustrations apply fictional technique as they are more emotional than those of the factual article.

The Slant

In determining the slant, keep in mind that the inspirational article is the poor man's psychiatrist. The key word of the slant is *self-help*.

1. *Market*

Because of the highly sentimental and emotional style, the best markets are magazines for women, teenagers, and religious or civic organizations. Recently, the digest markets have reprinted outstanding ones by well-known individuals.

2. *Subject*

The subject of these articles is any abstract concept, negative or positive, which poses a psychological problem. This problem must have strong reader identity. "The Worried Mind" is a negative concept while "The Gracious Receiver" is a positive one.

Other suitable subjects are: never say never, "thank you" is a good habit, the helpful hand, the forgiving heart, the contented mind, self-pity, the best you have. A good way to find these subjects is to think of the personality traits of your friends and acquaintances. Are they grasping, self-centered, generous, positive thinkers? Another means of finding suitable subjects is to use a thesaurus to find abstract words such as truth and honesty, or to read books of printed sermons for ministers.

3. *Length*

The best selling length is 1500 words, but those written by ministers run around 3500. Unless you have enough fuel for your fire, don't spread it too thin. In the longer lengths, you face the danger of becoming too unrealistic or too preachy.

4. *Viewpoint*

The article often begins in the first person with you-the-author relating a reader identity experience which coincides with the wrong image. Then the viewpoint transfers to the second person, *you.* The article can be written entirely in the second person, too. When the implied viewpoint is used, there is no shift. The better paying markets favor the implied viewpoint.

5. *Reader Reaction*

You want to inspire the reader to psychologically help himself to think positively. By showing the reader how you and others have faced the same depressing problem, you inspire him with the necessary confidence to solve his own problem.

6. *Immediacy*

The degree of immediacy varies with the problem. Some will demand immediate action while others prepare for the future. If the reader discovers that he has the negative trait, he must act at once to get rid of it. When the article discusses only the positive trait, the reader will act at the first opportunity.

7. *Red String*

The red string is the capsule sentence, but the reader identity problem and the inspiring emotion give support.

8. *Title*

The title usually refers to the psychological problem. Some writers put it in question form while others rely on a phrase or a statement. These titles generally are rather long. The working title is a word or phrase which states the problem, such as "worried mind."

9. *Author's Image*

You-the-author are a person who has faced such a problem and successfully solved it. Likewise, you have seen others successfully rise above this problem; so you wish to assist the reader in helping himself by sharing your experiences.

10. *Style*

The article consists of long rambling sentences and frequent quotations to gild the inspirational mood. From any book of famous quotations, you can find numerous literary references by checking under key words: giving, receiving, worry. Paraphrase quotations whenever necessary, but give credit to the author for the idea. The illustrations are written emotionally like fiction.

SLANT SHEET ON THE WORRIED MIND

1. *Market:* digest, religious, women's magazines

2. *Subject:* worry

3. *Length:* 1500 words

4. *Viewpoint:* I-you

5. *Reader Reaction:* inspirational confidence

6. *Immediacy:* now

7. *Red String:* capsule sentence, psychological problem, and emotion

8. *Title:* The Worried Mind

9. *Author's Image:* I have found the solution to this

problem, know others who have done likewise, and believe you can also

10. *Style:* literary and rambling

THE PATTERN

The pattern follows the basic formula but stresses the hook and the development. In writing this article, avoid becoming preachy or over-emotional.

1. *Hook*

The hook is lengthy, running three to four hundred words, and shows the wrong image or attitude toward the abstract problem. The best types of hooks are: action, summary, problem, definition, case history, character trait, literary quotations, statement of a person, comparison and contrast, or combinations of these basic hooks.

2. *Capsule Sentence*

The capsule sentence is long and rambling but always implies that you-the-author have found the right solution to the problem and that the reader can, too. You may use a paragraph or long literary quotation to lead up to the capsule sentence.

3. *Authority*

With the *I-you* viewpoint, the hook will show that you have been through this crisis and the development proves that you conquered it. In implied viewpoint, your illustrations involving the experiences of numerous individuals and the presentation of these are sufficient authority to prove that you are qualified to write on this subject. When a minister or priest writes this type of article, the by-line, blurb, or footnote states his authority.

4. *Development*

The development of a negative idea, such as the "worried mind," explains first the *when, where, what, who,* and *why* of the wrong image or attitude. Choose the W-words you need to explain the subject. The reader then diagnoses his negative case and is ready to learn the cure.

The other half of the development shows the reader how to overcome his wrong attitude or image in a step-by-step procedure. The reader must have no doubts as to the psychological plan. This special problem requires the *I-you* viewpoint.

If the problem is a fault common to everyone, you may follow the pattern of the idea article in which you solve the small problems. This automatically takes care of the larger or general problem. Naturally, you rely on the W-words to help you isolate the small problems. The choice of development depends upon your material: a specific or general problem. The general problem requires the implied or *you* viewpoint with illustrations from a wide variety of people.

The development of a positive concept, such as a gracious receiver, follows the development of the informative article. This structure, built around the W-words, requires less wordage but a strong plan. You create the image with descriptive adjectives and strong action verbs, then detail how the reader may acquire it.

The illustrations for all types of developments come from varied experiences of different people in order to give the psychological problem universality. Related only to each individual point it illustrates, the example is an emotional story of a person who made the right or wrong choice. The difficulty is citing enough negative illustrations for reader identity and plausibility but not so many that they revoke the effectiveness of the positive ones.

5. *Conclusion*

You have a choice of two conclusions. One type briefly enumerates the steps to accomplishment and encourages the reader to keep trying until he achieves. Between words of encouragement are interspersed literary quotations to give spiritual uplift.

The other type of conclusion relates a brief story which shows a character solving the problem with confidence. Incorporated in the action are the steps of accomplishment. This type of conclusion is difficult to write but adds a plus value to your article.

6. *Twist*

The twist emphatically leaves the reader with a final note of positive inspiration. If the conclusion ends with an illustration, the final inspirational words of advice are spoken by one of the characters.

WORK SHEET ON THE WORRIED MIND

1. *Hook:* The poet writes, "The little cares that fretted me, I lost them yesterday." This is more easily

said than done, and certainly no one knows it
better than I.

Last week I felt so ill I went to my doctor for
a physical check-up. A week later, I returned to
learn the results of the various tests. The doctor
studied his notes a second and then pushed them
to one side of the desk.

"What were your activities the week before
you came to see me?"

I thought a second. "On Tuesday I was in charge
of a luncheon for my club. It turned out all right
in spite of my fears. Friday, I drove a group of
Cub Scouts to the airport for a field trip. I was
never so relieved to arrive safely home with no
accidents. In fact, at the last minute I was so worried I almost cancelled out," I admitted.

"What else?" he asked quietly.

"Well, unexpected weekend guests, and I had
promised to handle the bake sale at the church
on Sunday morning. I felt terrible about leaving
them, and they will probably never forgive my
rudeness. At least the sale was a success, and I
was sure it wouldn't be," I concluded.

He looked grave. "The only thing I can find
wrong with you is a worried mind. If you want to
continue these activities, you must do them without fretting. Check your worries."

2. *Capsule Sentence:* There comes a time in life when
   everyone must put on the brakes and take inven-
   tory of himself. A little worry is healthy; but too
   much worry needs checking, and a positive course
   of action must be charted.

3. *Authority:* The authority is shown in the hook and the development.

4. *Development:*

> If you have a worried mind:
>> You review the past and blame yourself.
>>> Man in my neighborhood—scene—negative
>> You read hidden meanings into every spoken word or act.
>>> A famous person—narration—positive
>> You imagine the future and worry about it.
>>> A woman in my club—dramatic action—negative
>
> To get rid of a worried mind:
>> Force yourself to be calm.
>>> Historical situations—series of incidents—positive
>> Examine your fears sensibly.
>>> A person who could have misunderstood but didn't—narration—negative and positive
>> Accept the truth.
>>> A teacher I once knew—emotional reminiscence—positive

5. *Conclusion:* "Worry," according to George Washington Lyon, "is the interest paid by those who borrow trouble." The minute that worry creeps into your thoughts, stop right there and analyze the situation. As your worries vanish little by little, you will begin to think positively of the successful outcome of each undertaking.

6. *Twist:* Follow the example of Robert Jones Burdette who advises, "There are two days in the week about which and upon which I never worry. One is yesterday and the other is tomorrow." Soon you can add a third one—today.

Suggested Practice

Develop a work and a slant sheet for your inspirational idea. Note that you also state whether the examples are negative or positive in tone.

11.

Using Characterization to Strengthen an Idea

In the factual article the slight characterization appears in the illustrations and the projection of the author's image. For the fictional article, major and minor characters are projected as in a short story. You-the-author play the major role in two types of fictional articles. The other two provide only a minor viewpoint character role. In spite of the fact that the characterization is still not as strong as in the short story, you must know all the basic techniques of characterization.

CHARACTER TRAITS

A *trait* is an outward expression of the inner man, such as fairness, courage, determination. Exactly as in the short story, the article characters are flat in that you show only one dominant trait. The exception to this rule is the personality sketch where you project the major character round. In round characterization, you show several traits as in a novel or non-fiction book.

Only major characters are given traits. The major character differs from the supporting characters in that you project both the negative and affirmative sides of his trait to give him the illusion of roundness. The negative of courage is cowardliness. At the beginning of the article, the negative dominates. As the action proceeds, the major character moves toward the establishment of the positive trait. Such action in the article leads to the character *change*. The amount of change is equal to the difference between the negative and affirmative sides of the trait.

A character who is too impulsive and learns self-control has only a slight change. A person who steals and becomes honest makes a much greater change because there is more difference between his negative and positive traits.

With the exception of the nostalgic article, only the major character changes. To achieve the character change, you make the major character the focal center and line up the traits and tags of all supporting characters to accentuate the negative or affirmative of his trait. This arrangement produces the conflict of the article by providing the major character an opportunity to express his inner struggle outwardly.

You may select the character trait from one of four basic types.

1. *Image*

A trait which creates a picture of the major character for the reader is an *image*. Professions, nicknames, trades, geographical areas, and physical features are devices which photograph the major character. What image comes to your mind with these words: banker, librarian, Lizzie, grease monkey, Georgia cracker, okie, redhead, blonde, Midas, or Atlas? Give your major character an image trait when the action of the article is more important than the characterization. In other words, you create the action and then make the character fit it.

2. *Human*

If your story deals with a likable major character who does not realize that his little faults cause trouble for other people, you give him a *human* trait. "To err is human," the saying goes, and you excuse a person who means well but bungles, who tries to diet and sneaks a piece of candy. This trait emphasizes an excusable weakness or slight imperfection which any reader can understand, for he has it, too.

Do not use a weakness that is a criminal offense, like stealing, or one that is frowned on, like cheating. When you use an excusable weakness, the change consists of the major character recognizing the weakness and promising to correct it in the future.

3. *Ethical*

Every person has a code of morals, behavior patterns he

considers right and wrong. Since the degree of right and wrong behavior varies, express this trait in three different ways:

Excess Positive—Perhaps your character is so saving that he is frugal to an extreme. A virtue then becomes negative to produce the excess positive trait. For this trait, the change consists of reaching a positive balance.

Wrong Attitude—On the other hand, your character may think that saving for tomorrow is stupid and wants to live only for today. Then your character has a mistaken belief in regard to saving, a positive trait. This is the wrong attitude trait which changes by learning the truth. The amount of change depends upon the depth or strength of the mistaken idea.

Flaw—Any major character who lies, cheats, steals, or murders has a flaw. This is the worst type of ethical trait for the character must make a tremendous change. Because this change is so great, from black to white, the ending of the article implies the final change. The character knows he must change but realizes that this is not accomplished immediately but only after great effort.

4. *Distinctive Trait*

If no other person even remotely resembles your major character, he has a distinctive trait. As the old saying goes, the mold broke when he was born. The person who is different from anyone else must either conform or else maintain his trait against all attacks. Perhaps the character has extra-sensory perception. Either he uses it to a greater advantage or else he loses it completely.

Choose the human or excess positive traits when action and character development are equally important. If the wrong attitude trait is slight, use it this way, too. Whenever characterization is more important than the events of the article, apply the strong wrong attitude, the flaw, or the distinctive trait. In these, the amount of character change is equal to the degree of wrong attitude, flaw, or distinctiveness. The character change, however, is never as great as that in the short story.

Character Tags

Tags are visual or perceptive devices for quick recognition of a character. They reinforce and elaborate the dominant trait, giving the illusion of roundness and substituting for a trait of a minor character. Choose your tags from these basic ones.

1. *Action*

Any type of action the character performs gives the reader a picture. The character who walks with shuffling steps indicates age.

2. *Sensory*

A depiction by one or all five senses photographs the character. Blue eyes, a lilting voice, an exotic aroma, a satin skin, or a face filled with bitterness are a few examples.

3. *Background*

Background tags include a character's profession, the geographical area where he lives, his social status, his religion, or his education.

4. *Speech*

The way a character talks gives the reader a picture. The sound of his voice, the words he chooses, the way he pronounces his words are all speech tags.

5. *Mental*

The most important tag is the way a character thinks. Let him think quickly, slowly, in money terms, explosively, or dishonestly. Any one of these tags your character.

Character tags are not only used in the fictional article but are also excellent for projecting characters in the illustrations of your factual one.

CHARACTER MOTIVATION

The reader must know at all times why the characters behave the way they do in the action of the article. You-the-author decide how you want your characters to behave and then set up the proper motivation to explain such action to the reader. Before you can actually determine the motivation, you must first know how you want your reader to react toward your characters. Your major character is the key to motivation because all action in the article centers around him.

1. *Self-Identity or Escape*

If you want the reader to identify with the major character, let his life mirror the problems, setting, conflicts, and traits of the reader. The minor characters are those found in the reader's background. For self-identity motivation, give the major character an image, human, or excess positive trait.

When you motivate for escape, you select an exotic background but create the problem, the conflict, the emotion, and the other characters similar to those of the reader. The image or the distinctive trait provides the best escape identity.

2. *Sympathy or Plausibility*

With the wrong attitude trait, the reader is slow to identify with the negative of the major character. Likewise, the reader sees so few people who are rugged individualists that he has difficulty believing. In addition to taking the problem, setting, characters, and conflicts from the reader's life, you relate necessary incidents from the past, called *flashback,* to show how or why the character developed the wrong attitude or distinctive trait.

A story always opens on the day that is different. Anything which happened before this day is flashback. The flashback follows two forms: the interwoven or the solid. When you need little motivation to get the reader to believe or sympathize with a trait, a phrase or a sentence where explanation seems necessary is sufficient.

"*My father was the smallest boy in the family;* conse-

quently his sympathies were always with the underdog."
This italicized portion explains why father helped the needy.
Later you add, "Although he had long ago risen above
his underdog days, he could not resist a person needing
help." Three or four such statements lead the reader to
sympathize with father.

If the wrong attitude is practically a flaw or the distinctive
trait is almost impossible to believe, the solid flashback will
help you. Write it as a series of incidents, emotional reminiscence, dramatic action, narration, or a scene. Review
these devices in Chapter 7.

In the article, the flashback is brief, varying from one
paragraph to a page in length. The solid flashback, however, is long enough to show how the character developed
the mistaken idea or else to give proof that the distinctive
trait exists. Once you make the reader see the trait, he will
accept the character and enjoy the action.

3. *Understanding*

Any time your major character has a flaw, the reader
does not want to identify or sympathize with him. Through
a long, solid flashback, you make the motivating forces in
your character's life so degrading that the reader will understand the flaw.

When you have decided the way you want the reader to
react toward the major character of your article, line up
the supporting characters to help or hinder him in his efforts
to solve the problem. Lead the reader to like or dislike a
minor character through trait, tag, motivation, or viewpoint reaction. Since the reader identifies with the major

character, he will also accept the negative or affirmative reactions of the hero or heroine. In the article, the positive characters and decisions are stressed so strongly that the negative ones are mere shadows.

CHARACTER PROJECTION

When you show the reader a character rather than tell about him, you project. In the fictional article, most characters are projected in relation to the major character, the focal center of the action. You have a choice of several projection devices.

1. *By Speech*

A good rule to remember is that you are judged by what you say, so select the spoken words carefully. Compare the characters who spoke these words:

> "Success comes only with hard work."
> "Success is not what but who you know."

The words of the first character show he is a hard worker, but those of the second reveal a wheeler-dealer.

2. *By Action*

A child is often more perceptive than an adult because he observes the actions of a person. When you spank a child and tell him you love him, he is apt to say, "You don't act like it." Actions do speak louder than words. If you are a hard worker, your actions must reveal this.

3. *By Other Characters*

One character may say, "He's hard working, puts in twelve hours a day on the job." What one character says about another draws a picture for the reader.

4. *Viewpoint's Reaction*

By far the strongest device of projection in the article is the revelation of the viewpoint's thoughts or reactions. In the article, as in the short story, you enter the mind of only one person and share his thoughts with the reader. You cannot reveal the thoughts, other than by dialogue, of any other character. The viewpoint character in the article is you-the-author.

Thoughts are written in the same person as the viewpoint. With the exception of the personality sketch, you write in the first person, major or minor character. All thoughts are in the first person and must sound the way you talk in the dialogue. The personality sketch uses an implied viewpoint, so the thoughts of the major character are surmised by the viewpoint character.

Occasionally, you will write a humor article in the third person. When you reveal the thoughts of this viewpoint, they are written in the third person also. Changing the person of the viewpoint instantly marks you as a beginner.

Through thoughts and reactions, you easily shape the opinion of the reader in regard to the supporting characters and events. You may say, "I am suspicious of his intentions, but I will give him one more chance." You are telling the reader the character is not trustworthy. "I liked him the moment I saw him" keys the reader to like the character also.

5. *Others*

On very rare occasions, you may project a character with a document such as a letter, note, or advertisement.

> Wanted to Meet: Five feet six of blonde glamor. Do not recommend serious investment but avocation interest.
>
> After reading this, Amy was sure blondes live a more exciting life than brunettes.

This is a lazy way of projecting characters, so avoid it.

If you are poetic, let figures of speech project your characters. Think of some original ones—not such trite old expressions as: dry as a bone, blue as the sea, or bursting with curiosity.

Characterization is not easy, but it becomes less difficult with practice. Begin always with the major character, create the supporting ones to project the negative and the affirmative of his dominant trait.

Suggested Practice

Select the traits, tags, and motivation for the characters in your fictional articles. Write a short biographical sketch of each one so you will know them.

12.

How to Plan
a Personality Sketch

The personality sketch applies the characterization of fiction to the article formula. Either the flat characterization of the short story or the round of the novel are followed. The choice depends upon the versatility of the personality and the depth of the portrayal.

THE SLANT

The personality slant does not vary for a celebrity or an unknown who is doing a creditable job. When a personality has been done so many times, the difficulty is in finding a fresh approach.

1. *Market*

Personality sketches appear in almost all magazines. The

top women's magazines prefer famous personalities while the digests make no distinction. The religious preference is that the person be a Christian and possibly a member of the denomination which publishes the magazine. When a person is doing an outstanding job in foreign missions or on the home scene, editors are inclined to make an exception in regard to denomination.

Marketing the personality piece is a matter of common sense. The personality must have the same interests as the reader. Teenage magazines buy successful young personalities. Sport magazines want sports personalities; photography, photographers. Business publications prefer sketches of people who have the same interests as the reader.

2. Subject

The only restriction on subject is worthwhile achievement by the person who shares the reader's interests. Certainly hotrod readers are not interested in a personality sketch on a dress designer unless you focus on the fact he is a hotrod owner and racer.

3. Length

The personality sketch varies from 1500 words to 5000. The person and the market requirement establish the correct length for your article.

4. Viewpoint

The implied viewpoint is best because it keeps you as the line of communication between a personality and the reader—nothing more. First person viewpoint steals scenes from the star or clutters up the action. Since you take the reader on scene to see for himself, the implied viewpoint is more convincing.

5. *Reader Reaction*

The personality presented provides the emotion for the reader. You may want the reader to feel admiration, sorrow, laughter, or drama. If the public knows the personality as a comedian, the reverse picture showing the serious side is better. You may present the person as everyone knows him but with strong character projection.

6. *Immediacy*

The immediacy depends upon how much of the personality's life you intend to cover in your sketch. If you show a short, dynamic span of his total life, the immediacy is strong. A sketch which includes high points of a person's whole life or career has a vague immediacy. Remember that in a fictional article, immediacy covers the time period of the action.

7. *Red String*

The red string is the dominant trait or the philosophy of the personality. Assisting are the person's field of interest, setting, and emotion.

8. *Title*

The title refers to the trait and the occupation or avocation of the personality. Titles in men's magazines are more factual. The emotional and glamorous ones appear in women's magazines. The digest titles fall somewhere between the two extremes. The working title is the character trait or philosophy.

9. *Author's Image*

The author's image depends upon whether you like or dislike the personality. A sketch can crucify a person. Fortunately, you write about people you like or wish to defend.

10. *Style*

The reader wants to see and share the life of the personality, so you must show and not narrate. To show the personality requires dramatic scenes, strong characterization, and an emotional setting. The chief difficulty in writing is achieving a delicate balance between the truth and the fictional technique. While the reader wants to feel the emotion, at the same time he must believe that the facts really did happen.

SLANT SHEET ON THE OLD-TIME JOURNALIST

1. *Market:* digest, religious, men's magazines
2. *Subject:* old-time journalist
3. *Length:* 2000 words
4. *Viewpoint:* implied
5. *Reader Reaction:* admiration
6. *Immediacy:* vague
7. *Red String:* theme, newspaper background, and freedom trait

8. *Title:* Banner for Freedom

9. *Author's Image:* one who admires the journalist

10. *Style:* fictional

THE PATTERN

The character trait dictates the pattern. If the personality has several strong traits or has achieved in various fields of endeavor, you write him round. When you emphasize one field, the personality is flat. The presentation of the trait differs from fiction in that you stress the positive facet twice as much as the negative.

1. *Hook*

The fictional hooks are best in that they show the person. Most personality sketches open with a frame showing the person in action as he is today and his dominant trait. Then you go back and hit the high points of his life, ending with the final depiction of the opening, the person today. You are no doubt familiar with this teaser opening on television shows, starting at a high point and then going back to show how this was reached.

When the background plays an important role in shaping the personality, setting is a good hook. If the personality has overcome a great physical handicap or a difficult situation, open with the problem and person in action. Any time the personality has a strong philosophy of living, the theme hook is best. A combination of hooks, such as character-setting, is stronger than only one.

Do not overlook the factual hooks: summary, statement

of a person, comparison or contrast, shocker, case history, historical reference, reversal, and sometimes statistical. Whether you open with a factual or fictional hook, it must relate to the dominant trait of the personality.

2. *Capsule Sentence*

The capsule sentence states the dominant character trait as the author sees it.

3. *Authority*

The presentation of facts must imply that you know this personality and that your article is not a re-hash from other persons' presentations. Do not write about a person you have never met. This warning may seem unnecessary, but some beginners do try.

4. *Development*

The development relates the chronological story, stressing the dominant trait. Two types of developments are possible: the flat and the round.

If you do a flat characterization, you give the personality a strong dominant trait. To create roundness, you give him tags which elaborate the trait. Then you show the personality acting under different situations in chronological order but in only one field of interest. These situations are the decision points in the person's life or career.

When you show the character round, you rely upon the four basic traits as well as tags. With endeavors in a number of fields, you present his various images, such as musician, writer, director, and actor. Then you find some illustration of his human quality, of an ethical trait, and even of a distinctive trait. The tags reinforce these traits. One of these four traits must dominate.

A variation of the round pattern is the double development. You draw the personality round, then you go back into his past and show where, when, or how each trait began. Take the example above, where the dominant trait is the image. You state that he is a musician who has world acclaim, and you show him in action to prove this. Then you go back in his past and show how he practiced, who helped him, or perhaps his failing at his first concert. With the next trait, the excess positive, you overlay his image as a writer. Show that he works for absolute perfection and how this started in his youth.

His human trait of failing to learn his lines emerges with that of his actor image. Give an incident showing that in his youth he hated to learn lines. He has the distinctive trait of coordinating music, writing, and acting with directing. You illustrate this in the present and then show how the past experiences motivated it. Relating the events of the past chronologically gives unity to the sketch.

The factual structure is most important because this carries the line of truth. Hence, state the trait strongly so the reader will not miss it. The illustration shows emotionally the personality proving your statement. With the double development, you have an event from the present and the past giving proof.

The type of development influences the immediacy. The flat characterization is shorter and usually covers high points of the entire life, but not always. Since the round characterization takes more words, you stress a segment of the person's life unless the market will take 3500 or 5000 words. In the double development, you focus on the present and relate selected events from the past for emphasis. So you have two immediacies: the past and the present. The present is strong and the past vague.

To summarize, the fastest immediacy is a segment of life with a flat trait and the round trait next. The double development gives the impression of a fast immediacy because of the focus on the present. The slowest immediacy is the entire life and the flat trait.

The development also determines the length. The shortest, which makes up for the slow immediacy, is the flat trait with either the segment or the entire life. The round portrayal ranks next and finally the double development.

5. *Conclusion*

If you open with a frame hook, complete the action and stress the dominant trait. An anecdotal ending showing the dominant trait is a favorite. The ending must fit the personality.

6. *Twist*

The twist evokes a sob, a chuckle, or a challenging thought, depending upon the personality. He may make a statement, or the last line of the anecdote supplies the twist.

WORK SHEET ON THE OLD-TIME JOURNALIST

1. *Hook:* Ed Harvey placed the metal frame on the wooden table beside the alphabetical sections of

type. With unerring rapidity, he converted the
galleys into front page make-up of *The Banner*.
In a matter of hours, this four-paged weekly,
printed in a small Texas town, would begin its
journey to Americans in China, Europe, South
America, and other far-flung places.

2. *Capsule Sentence:* The reason for this wide circu-
lation is no secret to the subscribers. Ed Harvey
practices complete freedom of the press.

3. *Authority:* presentation of facts

4. *Development:*

> He devises his own rules for journalism.
>> advertisements on front page—narration
>> headlines for subscription renewals—quota-
>> tion from Ed
>
> Priority goes to local news no matter how un-
> important.
>> birth of babies—documentary
>> out-of-town visitors—narration and documen-
>> tary
>
> He re-writes national news from his own per-
> sonal slant.
>> world events—comparison and contrast
>> important people—dramatic action
>
> He publishes what he thinks.
>> hired hands in Washington—scene
>> crooked referee—incident

He has never raised the price of his newspaper or missed a deadline but owes no one.

politician who did not pay printing bill—series of incidents

shooting birds and golfing—narration

5. *Conclusion:* During World War II seasoned correspondents for world news syndicates voted Ed Harvey the editor they would most like to be and sent one of their members to present the award. The honor inspired the whole town to sponsor a special dinner for the presentation.

The presentation speech was short and simple but most sincere. The correspondent handed Ed the award.

6. *Twist:* Ed Harvey stared at the award for an intense moment. "This doesn't belong to me. I never took a journalism lesson in my life."

"Maybe not," the nationally known correspondent agreed, "but you've taught a number of graduate journalists the meaning of freedom of the press."

Suggested Practice

Devise a slant and a work sheet for your personality sketch. Choose any pattern which best projects your material.

13.

Articles
Need Plotting Too!

With the exception of the personality sketch, the fictional article adapts the characterization and plot formula of the short story to your facts. The adaptation has less conflict than the short story because the negative is not stressed as strongly as the positive and the scenes are weaker.

THE FORMULA

The four part formula confronts a character with a problem which he eventually solves by trial and error. Either you-the-author or another person is the major character.

1. *Critical Situation*

The story begins on the day that is different in the major

character's life. This day confronts the character with a problem which demands immediate action for a solution. Carefully select the problem so that it will be strong enough to carry the future action of the article, since all difficulties grow out of the problem.

A good way to test the problem is to list the future difficulties it will create. If you can list six or seven possibilities, you have a strong problem. To strengthen the problem further, set a time limit—the immediacy—after which the major character can take no further action.

As the critical situation develops, the reader must meet all characters by presence, name, or implication, and learn which will assist or deter the major character in his attempts to solve the problem. A character appearing in the critical situation may name another to appear later in the article. The mention of a club implies the president who comes in toward the end of the article.

In addition to introducing the characters, show the motivation of each so the reader will know who is for and who is against the major character. Develop the character conflict enough to assure the reader of future difficulties.

While you are introducing the characters and showing the problem and the conflict, you must let the reader know where and when the action takes place. The setting and time are woven into the action with a word or phrase here and there. All of these combine to provide the dominant emotion of romance or humor or tragedy. Stress the immediacy, if strong, to supply suspense.

In casting about for a remedy, the negative of the trait influences the character to choose one of several possibili-

ties for action. The critical situation ends with the decision
which involves the major character in a new problem. The
decision point gives the story forward movement—and suspense, if you let the reader know what the character expects to happen.

2. *Complications*

You reverse the expected to produce the new problem
or *complication*. From the decision in the critical situation
evolves the first complication. The decision at the end of
the first complication creates the problem in the next one.
Each positive decision for action moves the character a step
closer to his stronger or better self.

The number of complications controls the word length
of the article. However, when you let one problem create
too many complications, they become thin and unbeliev-
able. Three strong complications are better than six weak
ones.

Each complication takes place at a different time, moving
the action nearer to the limit you set. Keep the setting as
basic as possible by a central location and the surrounding
areas. Your article may take place in a home and the surrounding area.

3. *Crisis*

The worst and final complication is the crisis. The immediacy ends, and there is no more time for action. At this
point, the major character has a moment of revelation and
takes the final step in establishing his affirmative trait.
Action by the other characters brings about the moment

of revelation. Your character cannot "come to realize" the truth by positive thinking or by some other character relating a similar experience.

Here again, you firmly establish the time and show where the action takes place. You do not need a long description which stops the action of the article. Words and phrases woven into the action set the scene. The decision of the character to act in his affirmative trait is the character change and the end of the crisis.

4. *Climax*

In the climax, the major character acts twice in his affirmative trait to assure the reader of the change. In one short sentence he states or thinks what he has learned from the events. This is the *theme,* which every fictional article must have. Unlike the capsule sentence in the factual article, the theme comes at the end.

There are five pitfalls of plotting for a beginner: you select too weak a problem; each new complication does not grow out of the previous decision; you offer no choice for a decision by the major character; your major character does not change; and the theme does not fit the action or character change.

THE SCENE

Like the short story, the plot consists of scenes. A *scene* is a unit of action which expresses conflict between two or more characters. To write a scene, you follow the key W-words.

1. *Where*

Each scene has a certain place where the action is centered. When you move to a new area, you have a new scene. If you depict a location familiar to the reader and one which suggests conflict, you save wordage for more dramatic parts of the article. The place need not change with each scene.

2. *When*

The time always changes. A scene covers a short span of minutes or less than an hour. The shorter the time, the more dramatic is the impact. This urgency in time pushes the major character to act.

3. *Who*

In a scene, the viewpoint character is in action at all times with one or more of the other characters. He is either the major character who is the focal center of the action or a minor character who reports the action to the reader. In the article, you-the-author are the viewpoint character.

4. *Why*

Every scene has a purpose for being in the formula. Each character has a reason for being in the scene. If the scene or character serves no purpose in developing the action of the article, delete. You must let the reader know why each character is in the scene, to help or hinder the major character.

5. *What*

Every scene has two types of conflict: the inner conflict of the viewpoint character and the intensification of this in outer action with the other characters. Inner conflict consists of the viewpoint character's struggle between the affirmative and negative sides of his trait. You reveal this struggle to the reader through the viewpoint character's thoughts.

The viewpoint character's struggles with the other characters provide the outer conflict. When the viewpoint is that of a minor character, he reports the conflicts of the major character to the reader. Since you create your supporting characters either to agree or disagree with the major character, conflict is certain.

You express this outer conflict as: physical, mental, or emotional. Mental conflict consists of the characters' reasoning, arguing, explaining, or giving information to each other. In emotional conflict, the characters plead, beg, influence, or persuade. The characters may threaten violence or actually fight in physical conflict.

In all scenes except the crisis, use only one or two of these conflicts between characters but add variety by expressing the action in different ways. The characters in the critical situation scene may give information, explain, and argue for the mental, and plead, beg, and influence for the emotional conflict. The crisis is the only scene which presents the three conflicts in several different ways to make it the worst complication.

6. *How*

Hoping to solve the problem, the major character chooses a certain course of action at the end of the scene. This decision leads to the new problem of the next scene. The best way to understand the structure of the scene is to analyze one.

when	On Saturday morning at the break-
where, who	fast table my father unfolded the
	morning newspaper. "I see by the
information	headlines there's been another cy-
	clone in this area. I can't put off build-
	ing a cyclone cellar any longer." We
who	six children stopped eating when
	Mother set the coffee cup firmly in
	its saucer.
information	"Now, Ed, don't use a cyclone cel-
	lar for one of your brainstorms," she
	warned. Being a banker, Father was
	pretty good with figures, but Mother
	could out-figure him in other ways.
reason	"A man with six children needs to
	think of their safety," he reasoned.
argue	"You're only using this cellar as an
	excuse for one of your wild schemes,"
	she insisted. "And if you're picking
	out another worthless note to buy at
	the bank, why don't you get someone
reason	who can put in a watering system for

my rose garden?" She snapped her toast in two.

information   Father took great pride in the fact that his bank had never charged off a bad note. But he personally bought the bad notes at a discount and let the debtor work out the payments. He looked grim.

reason   "What would you do if a cyclone struck here in the next ten minutes?" At Mother's stunned silence, he continued. "My policy is always to

information   look ahead—not backwards with regrets."

information   "And whose worthless note have you decided to buy so you can help some waster?" she demanded. Father stood up, shocked and indignant.

decision   "I must get to the bank."

We knew the subject was far from settled because Mother grabbed her sunbonnet and retreated to her rose garden where she worked out her anger at Father. She grew the most beautiful roses in town.

When the action depicted is brief, substitute for a scene in the fictional formula one of the devices for illustrating a factual article. Never substitute in the crisis. Whether you use the scene or a substitute, dialogue is essential.

The Dialogue Pattern

In a scene, the dialogue shifts from full to bare or the reverse. *Full dialogue* consists of pointing to the speaker, the spoken word, and the "said" with reactions of the viewpoint character. *Bare dialogue* is the spoken word alone.

1. *Show the Speaker*

The reader must know at all times who speaks. To let a character talk before you introduce him only confuses the reader. At the end of a paragraph, point to the next speaker.

> We six children stopped eating when Mother set
> the coffee cup firmly in its saucer.

Mother will be the next one to speak.

Character tags are excellent devices to show the speaker. Viewpoint character reaction is another. Vary your devices to avoid monotony. By the time the reader is well-acquainted with the characters, the scene reaches a high peak of conflict and the spoken word sufficiently identifies the speakers.

2. *The Speaker Talks*

The spoken word carries the same emotion as the device which introduces the speaker.

> We six children stopped eating when Mother set
> the coffee cup firmly in its saucer.

"Now, Ed, don't use a cyclone cellar for one of
your brainstorms," she warned.

Mother is clearly getting ready for battle as shown in the
way she puts the coffee cup in the saucer. Her spoken words
carry the same bristling emotion. By repeating the emotion,
you intensify the conflict and tie the dialogue paragraphs
together.

Notice that the spoken word begins a new paragraph,
indicating that a different person speaks. This gives the
reader the illusion of more dialogue than there is. Readers
skip over long paragraphs of description and narration.

The spoken word must fit the character portrayed. When
strong-minded Father realizes that Mother has guessed his
true motive, he closes the argument.

Father stood up, shocked and indignant.
"I must get to the bank."

Since the spoken word reflects the immediacy of happening right now, write it in the present tense. For natural-
ness, the characters speak with fragmentary sentences,
broken off phrases finished with a gesture, dwindling words,
or interrupting exclamations. One character may complete
what another started to say or even reverse the meaning.
Each bit of dialogue must advance the conflict action.

To avoid loading the dialogue with information the characters already know, let the viewpoint character narrate
through thoughts—not spoken words—the facts the reader
needs to know.

Father took great pride in the fact his bank had never charged off a bad note. But he personally bought the bad notes at a discount and let the debtor work out the payments.

Listen to conversations and pattern your dialogue from them.

3. *The Speaker's Said*

The *said* carries the same emotion as the device indicating the speaker and the spoken word. The emotion shifts with the introduction of the new speaker.

"And whose worthless note have you decided to buy so you can help some waster?" she demanded. Father stood up, shocked and indignant.

Mother is accusing. Father is indignant, a shift in the emotion.

The intensity of the emotion projected in the scene depends upon the manipulation of the *said*. To say *he said* projects very little emotion. When you tell *how* he said, the emotion increases, as in *he said quietly*. A substitute for *said*, such as *he reasoned*, shows still stronger emotion. Drop the *said* entirely for the strongest emotion. By manipulating the *said* you create an up and down emotion in the scene.

In short, you are moving from full to bare dialogue or similar variation. As the conflict between characters increases, you shorten or drop the device pointing to the speaker. By the time the reader easily recognizes the characters, drop the viewpoint character's reaction and finally the *said* at the crisis point of the scene. This variation in dialogue intensifies the emotional conflict and gives the action forward movement.

Professional dialogue is not written in one draft but requires a good deal of revision. Knowing the dialogue pattern will shorten the revision period.

Suggested Practice

Construct a scene for any one of your fictional ideas.

14.

Writing
the Personal Experience

The chief competitor of the commercial short story is the personal experience article. The style varies from a factual account of events related exactly as they happened to an emotional one which combines the forcefulness of truth with the dramatic presentation of fiction.

The factual experience reports chiefly action, as in a hunting trip, while the emotional one puts the emphasis on character development, such as facing blindness. The best reader identity experience falls between these two extremes, giving character and action equal importance.

THE SLANT

The slants for the two extremes differ mostly in subject and style; consequently they provide the key words of *factual* and *emotional*.

1. Market

The emotional experience goes to digests, women's magazines, and the religious market. The digests are always seeking dramatic or exciting experiences. A particular one publishes three such experiences under separate feature titles each month. Two top women's magazines have a monthly feature in which they invite the reader to share her personal experiences dealing with family problems. Experiences of missionaries, priests, or ministers are popular with editors of religious magazines.

The factual experience goes to magazines for men as a sporting, photography, science, mechanics, general, or outdoor article. Business publications prefer experiences relating to interesting enterprises. A person may share his experiences of building a million dollar playland from a single shooting gallery.

The reader identity experience goes to teenage markets and home service magazines. These are closely related to the how-to-do-it article but deal strictly with a personal experience which the reader does not want to duplicate.

2. Subject

The subject determines the type of experience. The factual experience includes: hunting, collecting as a hobby, traveling, redecorating, camping, fishing, building a hobby into a small business, or landscaping a backyard.

The emotional experience covers family problem situations, teaching in a slum area, the struggle to become an actor, facing a physical handicap, taking part in a historic disaster, or putting Christian direction or deeper meaning in life.

The reader identity experience takes its subject from everyday living: raising ten children on a small salary, dieting, improving your personality, learning to be a public speaker, and other personal problems.

3. *Length*

The subject and the market determine the length. The wordage varies from 2000 to 5000. The longer length requires a strong problem which changes the whole direction of your life.

4. *Viewpoint*

All personal experiences are written in the first person, subjective viewpoint. Third person loses the reality and impact of truth, and the experience reads more like fiction than fact. If the experience is not your own, you still tell it in the first person. You by-line the story with the name of the person who experienced it and either add your name as coauthor or "as told to" you.

5. *Reader Reaction*

The experience dictates the dominant reaction from your reader. You-the-author can evoke thought, excitement, sympathy, admiration, or laughter.

6. *Immediacy*

The immediacy is the time period in which the experience takes place. When the experience takes place over a weekend or a week, the immediacy is strong. In the factual experience the immediacy can provide suspense, as in the case of a hunter who has only a week to shoot his elk.

The reader identity and the emotional experience usually cover a long period of time. You give a false immediacy by depicting only the emotional high points of the time. Many end on the implication that you have found the solution and will use it from now on.

7. *Red String*

The red string in the factual and reader identity experience is the capsule sentence, such as "I lost 80 pounds" or "I collect old guns." Characterization, setting, and emotion give support along with viewpoint.

The viewpoint is the red string in the emotional experience. Reinforcing the viewpoint are: character trait, setting, emotion, and theme.

8. *Title*

While titles vary with markets, they all stress the *I*. Women's magazines and digests seem to favor symbolic titles which highlight the results. Men's markets use factual titles. The working title emphasizes the results of the experience also.

9. *Author's Image*

The image varies with the experience. If the experience tells of hunting in Africa, the author is a big game hunter. Perhaps a teenager relates her experiences participating in the Olympics.

10. *Style*

The factual account is mostly narration or in diary form. The narration uses action verbs and short sentences to project excitement.

You write the emotional experience dramatically, as in a short story. While the plot structure must follow the truth, the characterization and events are highly dramatized to project the experience to the reader.

The reader identity experience strongly resembles the styling of the idea article, a tight balance of fact and fictional technique. The style differs in that the reader of the idea article expects to use the information, but the reaction to the experience article is practically the same as to a short story—entertainment.

The example of this type of article is a reader identity experience in "as told to" format.

SLANT SHEET ON WIDOW GOING TO COLLEGE

1. *Market:* religious, digest, or women's magazines

2. *Subject:* housewife and widow goes to college

3. *Length:* 2000 words

4. *Viewpoint:* first person as told to author

5. *Reader Reaction:* inspiration

6. *Immediacy:* three years

7. *Red String:* viewpoint, character trait, setting, theme

8. *Title:* My Husband's Legacy

9. *Author's Image:* a housewife and recent widow, mother of two teenage girls

10. *Style:* truth dramatized

THE PATTERN

The pattern follows the formula of the short story, but the dramatic impact varies with the type of experience. It differs from the short story in that more complications are included and affirmative decisions greatly outnumber the negative ones.

1. *Critical Situation*

The critical situation hooks the reader, shows when and where the experience takes place, introduces the viewpoint character's problem, promises conflict, provides character motivation, and forces a decision for action.

HOOK: The factual article hooks the reader with: summary, capsule sentence, problem, case history, or action. The emotional article favors character trait, setting, or theme, depending upon which is stressed the most in the experience. The material determines whether the reader identity experiences use the factual or the fictional hooks.

To make the experience believable, numerous details are included. Since these details slow the pace, the frame hook adds suspense and immediacy to the experience. Open the article at a point immediately before the final results, projecting that exciting moment. Do not give the final results but go back to the beginning and chronologically develop the experience. In the example, Amy has been offered employment at the salary which will more than support her family, and then Dean Harris proposes marriage. This is a favorite hook with all types of personal experience.

TIME AND PLACE: The critical situation not only tells the reader when the action begins but also states how long it will last. This is true in all experiences.

Most experiences take place in a basic setting, as a home, college campus, or a territory for hunting. The other action revolves around this central location.

PROBLEM: In the first paragraph the critical situation lets the reader know the problem. The problem may grow out of the setting, the character trait, or the explosive situation. The problem for the factual experience comes mostly from setting or situation. The emotional experience is based on a character trait problem while reader identity uses all three sources to create the problem.

CONFLICT: The conflict in the factual experiences arises from setting, fighting the forces of nature, or from situations created by minor characters. The emotional experience emphasizes strong inner conflict from the trait and outer conflict with supporting characters. The conflict of the reader identity experience falls half-way between the two extremes with both inner and outer struggles created by both the trait and the situation.

MOTIVATION: The factual experience requires the least motivation. Always to dream and plan to go big game hunting is sufficient. In the reader identity experience, the reader must know what caused the problem in order to believe. The motivation is strongest in the emotional experience because it deals with a specialized problem which needs sympathy or understanding. The factual experience often provides escape; the next one, reader identity; and third, strong emotional release.

DECISION: The decision in the factual account is slight and almost pre-determined, a recounting of what happened next. With the emotional experience, the decision grows out of the problem and the conflict. While the reader identity experience is more or less pre-determined, the fictional treatment intensifies the problem and the conflict to project the illusion of the decision happening now. In both the reader identity and the emotional experience, the decision creates the new complication.

2. Complications

The short story has one or three complications, but the personal experience has any number to stress the positive movement toward achievement. The only limit to the number of complications is the importance of the experience. The complications in the factual experience are a narration of the true events, eliminating those of lesser importance.

In the emotional and the reader identity experiences the decision leads to the next complication. You minimize the negative or wrong decision by stressing or showing the positive action.

3. *Crisis*

In the factual account, the crisis shows the peak of attainment. You-the-viewpoint must find the solution to your problem in the reader identity and emotional article crisis. Conflict with other characters brings about the moment of revelation.

The character change is very slight in the factual account; the experience has been achieved. In the emotional experience, the change gives new direction; the viewpoint character learns to accept blindness. Again, the reader identity experience has more change than the factual but less than the emotional. In the example, Amy changes from a grieving widow with little education to an educated bride of a college dean.

4. *Climax*

The factual experience winds up quickly; the hunter packs up and goes home. In the reader identity experience, the viewpoint character acts in his new image and relates the theme. You actually narrate these climaxes to give the emotional effect of talking to the reader directly for a ring of truth.

The viewpoint character in the emotional experience follows the short story in that he acts twice to establish his change of character. The theme, however, is spelled out in soliloquy fashion, wringing out every drop of emotion and leaving nothing to the reader's imagination. This climax is almost double the length of that in the other two types of experiences.

Any time the character trait is a flaw, the experience shows the viewpoint character trying to change but not completely accomplishing the change. The hopeful note in the soliloquy assures the reader of the eventual accomplishment of the change.

Work Sheet on My Husband's Legacy

1. *Critical Situation*

HOOK: That July afternoon the trailer was like an oven, but I was not aware of the heat. The man from Joe's construction company mopped his red face as he squeezed into one of the small trailer chairs.

"You're more fortunate than most widows. Joe's accidental death gives you his full salary for three years." He fumbled with the clasp of his brief case. "If you want to sell this trailer—"

"No—never!" This was our home and must keep on being home to my two daughters. Besides, the trailer was the only way I knew of keeping Joe with me.

TIME AND PLACE: The trailer is the basic setting. The accidental death benefits gave me Joe's full salary for the next three years. Experience begins in July.

PROBLEM: I married Joe before I finished high school, and I had no training which would enable me to get a job and support my two teenage girls.

CONFLICT: Lynda, who planned to enter State University in the fall, was even less qualified than I to support herself. Debbie would be a freshman in high school. I wanted the girls to go to college, and I needed training which would enable me to send them and, later in life, not to burden them for support.

MOTIVATION: Joe had assured both girls he would see that they had a college education. Now that Joe was gone, I must keep his promise.

DECISION: I decided to move the trailer we owned to State University and use the money to go to college with my daughter. By attending summer school, I could finish in three years.

2. Complications

I learned that I could not qualify for entrance on credits because I did not finish high school. I went to Dean Harris who permitted me to enter on individual approval.

Lynda and I registered in different classes, but I had trouble studying; it had been so long. Dean Harris arranged for me to have a tutor. I paid for his services by doing his laundry and mending.

My grades were good enough to get me off probation after the first year. I had been so busy I did not notice that Lynda was dating less and less. She finally confessed that the boys had the wrong opinion of her because we lived in this trailer camp. Dean Harris arranged for us to move to College Villa, a trailer park for married students.

In summer school, my daughter and I were put in the same swimming class. I was overweight and an embarrassment to her. The Dean arranged for me to take swimming with the faculty wives.

The second year, I missed Joe even more. My studies came easier, and I was better organized at home. Lynda and Debbie were busier. Then Debbie needed a father for the annual dads and daughters affair. I asked Dean Harris if his wife would object. He accepted and explained he was a bachelor. Later, I invited him to dinner, and he returned the invitation.

I had chosen homemaking as my major, so I, along with other junior students, assisted with the graduation tea at the end of the summer. By accident I learned that I was the subject of campus gossip for the way I was trying to catch Dean Harris. I found so many excuses not to see him that he finally stopped trying to see me.

During my final year, I was making all A's, wore a size fourteen dress, and was very lonely. I kept trying to recall the old "me" and Joe, but the memory faded. In the spring Lynda became pinned to my former tutor. I started making applications for teaching positions. Debbie was running with a group that was a little too ready to live. I began to restrict her freedom.

3. *Crisis*

We quarrelled violently the Saturday night I kept her home. Her crowd broke into a summer cottage and completely demolished the furnishings. Debbie was taken to the police station for questioning as she had been going with the crowd. I called Dean Harris, and he saw that Debbie was cleared of any charges.

When he brought her home, he demanded to know why I had discontinued our friendship. I confessed about the gossip. He asked me to share his life. That very day I had been offered a teaching position. I was ready to support myself and my girls, but they needed a father and I needed a husband.

4. *Climax*

I married Dean Harris. The woman who loves Dean Harris is not the same one who loved Joe. I feel sure that Joe knows and approves of the way I handled his legacy. All Joe ever wanted was to make me and the girls happy.

You convert the narration of the plot summary into scenes and scene substitutions before you write your first draft.

Suggested Practice

When you have completed your plot summary for your first person idea, outline the parts in scenes and scene substitutes, ready for the first draft.

15.

Emotionalizing
the Nostalgic Article

The nostalgic article emotionally remembers a person, place, or situation from the past and shares these personal reminiscences with the reader. In the factual pattern, the past usually seems better than the present.

The Slant

The slant for the nostalgic article is practically the same for both the factual and the fictional pattern.

1. Market

The religious and digest markets are rather consistent in publishing this type of article. In the women's and home service market, the article runs in cycles of popularity. Occasionally, this type of article appears in business publi-

cations, house organs, professional journals, or magazines
of civic organizations. The nostalgic article is seen in men's
magazines as memoirs of old game hunters, law enforce-
ment officers, or people who have lived with excitement.

2. Subject

The good old days are constantly changing with each
new generation, so the subjects are unlimited. Any person,
place, or thing which no longer appears in present-day
civilization is a subject for the nostalgic article.

One person suggests an entire class, such as: the old time
druggist, the traveling photographer, the itinerant oculist,
the country doctor, or the hired girl. You may recall silent
movie houses, attics, or two room schools. Perhaps you prefer to recall more personal things, like the ice cream socials
at the church, hay rides, beauty aids for freckles, old time
remedies for diseases, or odd superstitions.

3. Length

The length varies from 1500 to 2000 words for the digest
or women's market. The shorter length is easier to sell
because it is difficult to keep the reader in the past too
long and hold his attention.

4. Viewpoint

You have a choice of two subjective viewpoints: participating major character or reporting minor character. Although you report the action from the viewpoint of a
youngster, you are an adult relating the situation as you
remembered this in your childhood. This is not the same as

the viewpoint of a child participating in the events as they happen and being part of them. The nostalgic article action has already happened, and you retell it from memory as an adult.

5. *Reader Reaction*

You want the reader to remember nostalgically and to identify with your past. This is also appealing to the escapist who is too young to remember and identify himself.

6. *Immediacy*

The immediacy is unimportant. The article may cover several hours, months, or years. There is no strong urgency to take action to solve a problem.

7. *Red String*

The red string in the factual pattern is the capsule sentence, but the fictional piece relies on viewpoint, character trait, and theme. Setting also strengthens the continuity.

8. *Title*

The title is rather vague in meaning, containing nostalgic or old-fashioned expressions which characterize the age but relate to the subject. Frequently, the title is a phrase one of the characters keeps saying. The theme or the capsule sentence is the working title.

10. *Style*

To maintain the nostalgic mood, you sprinkle in words like: remember, recall, cannot forget. Although the article is heavily illustrated with action, the pace is very slow because of viewpoint narration in long rambling sentences.

Slant Sheet on Cyclone Cellar

1. *Market:* digest, religious, women's magazines

2. *Subject:* Father builds a cyclone cellar

3. *Length:* 1500 words

4. *Viewpoint:* I the reporter

5. *Reader Reaction:* humorously nostalgic

6. *Immediacy:* one year

7. *Red String:* Father's trait of faith in people and the cyclone cellar

8. *Title:* The Improbable Occurrence

9. *Author's image:* a younger member of a large family

10. *Style:* fictional treatment

The Pattern

The nostalgic article follows two patterns: the factual criticism of present-day times and the fictional pattern of the unforgettable person, place, or event. The factual criticism opens with a present-day situation, then in the capsule sentence compares it to a similar one in the past.

The development enumerates and illustrates the points where the past was better than the present. The conclusion and the twist bring the present back into focus. Since you have already done five work sheets of this type, you will want to learn the fictional pattern of the nostalgic article.

1. *Critical Situation*

HOOK: The type of fictional hook depends upon the focus of the article. An action hook showing the problem puts the emphasis on situation. Open with the trait in conflict to stress character dominance. A setting or theme hook creates a special nostalgic mood. You may want to combine trait with theme or setting with action. Some material requires the frame hook for the proper nostalgic mood.

TIME AND PLACE: The immediacy varies from one day to a year, depending on your material. The passage of time, however, is clearly indicated to counteract the slow pace.

Like the short story, you establish a basic setting and try to keep the scenes in or around this location. So, in the critical situation you set the place sharply in the reader's mind; then key words will project it in later scenes. The description of setting and of the specific period in your past are interwoven through action and the viewpoint character's thoughts.

PROBLEM: The reader must know what the problem is and how difficult it is to solve. When you use the viewpoint character as an observer of the events, the problem belongs to the major character. The observer, however, is involved in the action of the story and appears in every scene in order to keep the reader aware of how the major character tries to solve his problem.

CONFLICT: Rarely does the nostalgic article involve conflict with nature or the setting. There is little inner conflict when a minor character reports the events, but a large amount of outer conflict between characters. The minor viewpoint character surmises what the major character thinks.

If the major character is the viewpoint, his thoughts produce much of the nostalgic mood as well as the inner conflict. The conflict with characters provides the other half.

MOTIVATION: Each character is motivated, but not too strongly. The surface motivation lets the reader know what each character wants. This information is a matter of well-placed sentences here and there as needed. If the nostalgic memory is a bitter one for the major character, he needs some strong motivation.

DECISION: You offer the character a choice of action, and he chooses the course which will keep the conflict going. This decision leads to the first complication. The major character always makes the decision.

2. *Complications*

The number of complications designates the length of the article. Each complication grows out of the previous decision which makes the original situation worse. Hence the strength of the problem or the character trait along with the market requirement limit the number of complications.

3. *Crisis*

The crisis is the worst and final complication in the chain of events. The immediacy or time limit has arrived. This article differs from the regular fictional formula in that the major character does not change. At the moment of revelation, created by character action, the supporting characters change to accept the wisdom of the major one.

4. *Climax*

The climax relates the final incidents and sums up the action with a theme. A minor character, the viewpoint character or the one in conflict with the major one, states the theme.

WORK SHEET ON THE IMPROBABLE OCCURRENCE

1. *Critical Situation*

HOOK: Success to my father was proving that nothing was impossible. He referred to this as practicing the possible. In our small West Texas town, no one, not even Mother, took stock in his belief. She called it practicing the impossible and had developed an extra-sensory perception which almost instantly detected Father's outlandish projects, such as the cyclone cellar.

TIME AND PLACE: The action takes place in and around a home in a small West Texas town during the 1920 era. The immediacy is one year, from May to May. Father and Mother have the first quarrel over the cyclone cellar at the breakfast table.

PROBLEM: Under the guise of building a cyclone cellar, Father wants to help three men find themselves.

CONFLICT: Father must overcome Mother's opposition, the weaknesses of the three men, and the attitude of the entire town.

MOTIVATION: Father's past successes, in finding the best in men, spurs him on. He also wants to protect his children from cyclones. Mother will go along if she gets a better rose garden. The men get a taste of success.

DECISION: Father ends the discussion by saying he must get to the bank. Mother retreats to the rose garden to work out her anger at Father.

2. *Complications*

Father asks the brightest teacher on the high school faculty to find mathematically the safest spot for the cellar in our backyard. The choice was Mother's rose garden. Father promises to hire the best man in town to move the rose bushes and make her a formal garden.

Father buys the bad note of the best nurseryman in town, now hopelessly in debt, and hires him to do the rose garden and work out his note. Father also buys the note of the town drunkard and hires him to build the cellar.

Mother insists the cellar will never be built and proceeds to harass Father when the man comes to work drunk or does not come at all. By this time the whole town has become interested in the banker's folly, but Father strongly encourages the teacher to apply for a teaching position at the State University.

By September the teacher leaves to join the faculty at the University. Father encourages the man who built Mother's garden to come to the house and explain his work each Sunday when the town comes visiting the cellar. He takes orders from the guests.

When winter comes, the contractor has stopped drinking, but he has to wait until spring to pour the concrete. Father assures everyone that the cellar will be finished in time for the first cyclone, and he trains us in first aid and in alerting the neighbors. Each child has an assigned duty.

In April the cellar is finally finished. The neighbors donate furnishings. Mother holds an open house and gives away her roses after a tour of the garden. The contractor and the nurseryman are on hand to take orders. The teacher wires congratulations which Father reads and also a clipping from the newspaper which states that our Professor has won a special mathematics award.

3. *Crisis*

Everyone awaited the cyclone to find out if the cellar would really prove storm-worthy. We waited, too, anxiously, to perform our duties of alerting the neighbors and providing any first aid. When the cyclone came, it arrived minutes before midnight. The neighbors woke us; they had performed all our assigned duties.

When Father was sure the storm had passed on, he and the other men tried to raise the door. Eventually, they cleared the trap door for escape, and Father climbed through it. He cleared enough debris for the men to open the large door. We came out of the cellar praising Father for his farsightedness.

4. *Climax*

Out of the cellar, we surveyed the damage done by the

cyclone. Mother screamed with delight. Her rose garden, for some freakish reason, had not been touched.

Father had practiced the possible, but Mother explained it as an impossible belief in the occurrence of the improbable.

Suggested Practice

When you have completed your slant and work sheets on your nostalgic idea, the next step is to spell out the plot summary in scenes or substitutes. Put each scene or substitute outline on a separate page so you can check the time through each one, the place, and so on through all the parts.

16.

Make Your Humor Amusing

Exaggeration sells the humor article, which utilizes the patterns of both the article and the fiction formula. Written in fiction, this article is the chief competitor of the short-short story. The satire conforms to any of the article patterns except the inspirational. Do not confuse the true humor article with one which contains humorous parts.

THE SLANT

Regardless of which pattern you choose, the slant varies little. The key is healthy humor.

1. *Market*

Well-written humor articles are always salable. Women's magazines usually prefer articles by known writers. Home service, religious, and digest markets buy the article rather than the author's name. Business and organization publications are publishing more humor than formerly.

Unfortunately, the filler market and columnists are constantly encroaching on the humor article. Written by contributors, the fillers are lumped together with a hook and a red string for a monthly feature and substitute for a humor piece. Several magazines have writers under contract for a monthly humor feature. Quality magazines have special sections for humor.

2. *Subject*

The only restriction on humor is good taste. Human relation situations which suggest humor are those between husband and wife, spouse and mother-in-law, parent and child, guest and host, boss and employee. Conflict is in doing a task or personal reactions to a political situation, headline news, or scientific improvements. Do not overlook customs and traditions.

Humor easily becomes a two edged sword: a laugh on one side and a sharp jab on the other. Laughter is a good way to point out a defect of which many people are aware, but personal animosities make stale humor. Furthermore, some subjects are not laughing matters, such as Christmas or Easter. Keep the subject of your humor healthy, and you will sell.

3. *Length*

Humor becomes strained or goes sour if sustained too long. The salable length is from 1000 to 1500 words. Magazines which have special humor sections will buy pieces around 800 words.

4. *Viewpoint*

The subject and the pattern suggest the viewpoint. When you write satire, the implied viewpoint, never identifying yourself, is best for the informative, idea, controversial, or personality sketch. The how-to-do-it favors the *you*.

The personal experience requires an *I*, the major character viewpoint. The first person viewpoint in the nostalgic piece is either a minor or major character.

When the pattern follows the humor situation or character trait, you may choose either the first person major or minor character viewpoint. The problem and the conflict will help you choose the major character so you can determine the viewpoint.

5. *Reader Reaction*

Every humor piece must make the reader laugh primarily, but this is not the only reaction. Most humor articles also ridicule human actions and point out needs for change. This is especially true of satire. While you exaggerate the situation, the reader must have enough of the facts to see the truth. So most humor articles carry a serious reaction under the cover of laughter.

6. *Immediacy*

In satire, the immediacy refers to when the reader will use the information. You follow the immediacy of the pattern of the factual article you choose. For satire in the fictional article, the immediacy refers to the length of time covered by the action. Usually this is very vague.

When you follow the short story formula exactly, the immediacy is the span of time from the critical situation to the character change. The immediacy in the character trait formula is rather indefinite, but the one in the situation is frequently strong for humorous suspense.

7. *Red String*

The red string follows the dictates of the pattern you choose for your material. The factual pattern emphasizes the capsule sentence while the fictional and short story format rely on the trait, viewpoint, theme, and others.

8. *Title*

The working title for the factual patterns is a short form of the capsule sentence while in the fictional pieces either the character trait or the theme provide a descriptive phrase.

The final title is a clever twist of words or a pun like "Quick on the Drawl" or "Tomorrow We Diet." Whenever possible, give a quick preview of the subject or character action. You will usually find the title in some phrase in the article.

9. *Author's Image*

The general image is anyone who has a healthy sense of humor and who can laugh at himself. The specific image varies with the material: a housewife, a husband, a scientist, a citizen.

10. *Style*

The satire varies in style. Some are slow, labored in pace, winding in and out of the points to develop. Others have a breezy style. You tend to develop certain characteristics which stamp your style with your identity.

The fictional piece moves at a very fast pace, almost breathtaking at times. Fast pace comes with short scenes which end on implication. Rather than spell out the results, you simply state, "After I escaped from that situation." Puns and clever twists on words add to the lightness of style.

Formats, long discarded by the short story writer, will sell here. You may write the piece as a diary, a series of letters, inter-office communication, advertisements in the newspapers, questions and answers in an interview, or fill-ins of a questionnaire. Style is paramount in the humor article; editors demand that you create your own.

THE SATIRE PATTERNS

Seven of the article patterns previously discussed adapt to satire, in that you write seriously on an absurd subject to produce the humor.

1. *Informative*

To convert the informative pattern into a satire, you select a serious or made-up subject and give nonsense information. Instead of giving major facts, you stress unimportant ones, inventing authorities to quote, coining academic words, and drawing ridiculous conclusions.

Suppose you want to distinguish between liberals and conservatives. You say that liberals wear flashy clothes while conservatives dress inconspicuously. Conservatives drink tea, but liberals choose coffee because it is more plentiful. Your final conclusion is that liberals have large families; therefore there are more liberals than conservatives.

2. *How-To-Do-It*

In a how-to-do-it satire, you write tongue-in-cheek on the reverse of an accepted attitude: how to be poor, how to be nervous, or how to become psychotic. Reverse the accepted procedure, such as how not to build a patio. Numbering the steps needed to accomplish a task is a favorite format. In discussing the six easy steps to becoming a columnist, stress the unimportant things: coining words, making up clever subtitles, or having big ears. Another type is five easy steps to staying single, but you admit it didn't work for you.

3. *Idea*

To create satire from the idea pattern, relate the practical facts but show the impractical results in the illustrations. This misapplication of facts and unnecessary substitutions produce the humorous results.

Take the subject, "People Should Know First Aid." The facts state good first aid principles, but your misapplication through interpretation and substitution produce disastrous results to create the laughs.

Another humorous angle is to suggest a needed invention.

You can suggest time savers for overworked mothers, or crisis meters for the worrier, reminders for the absent minded, the automatic cut-off for telephone conversations, television, and guests who won't leave. Any impractical solution to a problem in everyday living is suitable for this type of humor.

4. *Controversial*

One humorous approach to the controversial subject is to choose a subject which is not debatable and make it argumentative. By advocating the abolition of a necessity, such as getting rid of the automobile, is one device. Your arguments are: people will stay home, learn about each other and no longer be strangers, live on less money, have fewer family quarrels.

You may quote legislation before congress and suggest an amendment which is pure nonsense. Suggesting new taxes to balance the budget is always a good source of humor. A father points out why he proposes a luxury tax on bachelors, or a housewife urges a labor tax on career women. These pet peeves with strong reader identity are elevated to the importance of national legislation.

5. *Personality Sketch*

In doing a humorous personality sketch, elevate a minor trait to great importance. A personality is outstanding because he can wiggle his ears. Another approach is to create a personality and impressively compare his unimportant contributions to those of famous people. Monologues of comedians frequently follow this format.

On the other hand, you may exaggerate a normal trait in a person to such an extreme that it becomes hilarious. Take the trait of being unable to resist a salesman. You brag about all the useless items you have purchased. You may describe the irrational inventions of the personality.

The multi-personality sketch emphasizes the various types of people in a special group. You show bores to avoid, friends you could do without, or traveling companions to evade. The last paragraph of the series shows you-the-author as a composite of all types.

6. *Personal Experience*

The humorous personal experience differs from the personality sketch in that the situation is as important as the character. Current affairs suggest the factual account or the reader identity experience, but imagination provides the events.

Today practically everyone has several numbers by which he is known: social security, telephone, armed forces, or zip code. You may give a humorous account of your experiences with wrong numbers. Your experiences saving trading stamps offer another possibility. Create a country and people, and then relate your adventures.

7. *Nostalgic*

With this pattern you choose to remember what no one deems worthy to recall. You remember the delicious cakes your mother made from ready-mixes. You look at the ultramodern in cars and point out how far short it falls by comparison to a sport model of the 1920 era. Humor comes from seriously remembering the ridiculous.

In writing satire, never hesitate to combine patterns. Personality sketch blends with nostalgic, personal experience with controversial, or idea with nostalgic. Devising individual patterns to fit your material is the creative process.

The Fiction Formula

The fictional adaptation of the humor article differs from the short-short in that the characterization is not as strong and the scenes are shorter with less conflict. The climax generally implies that the whole cycle of events will begin again. Each new complication grows out of the previous decision.

1. *Character Trait*

Give the major character an exaggerated trait and show how it creates the critical situation and the series of complications. The first sentence states the trait: "I am incident prone." Then you show that no matter what you do, an incident becomes an international crisis in your life.

As a result of the final crisis, you resolve to be more cautious in the future. In the climax, a new situation confronts you, similar to the opening one, and the implication is that the cycle of events will start again.

The joke is always on the viewpoint character, even though he is not the major character. The narrator sets out to prove that his wife is not a mind reader although she predicts future events. He is sure she has a secret source of information. He checks on various possibilities of how she gets the information and finally thinks he knows the secret. He rushes home to confront her with the knowledge, and she reads his mind before he can say a word.

2. *Problem-Action*

The viewpoint character, in trying to solve a simple problem, becomes involved in a series of humorous complications which compound the difficulty. Suppose you have a face that always looks familiar. You open the piece with, "The trouble with my face is that people seem to think they have seen it before."

In a grocery store a woman insists that you are the missing witness her lawyer has been hunting to testify about an accident. You are ordered to appear in court, but you swear that you did not witness the accident. Since you cannot prove you were not at the scene of the accident or any other place, the judge threatens to fine you for perjury. The lawyer accuses you of being bought by the other party.

Your wife threatens to divorce you unless you can explain what you were doing in that part of town where the accident occurred. Your boss wants an explanation. You decide to admit you were the witness but do not remember any of the details of the accident.

Then the real witness appears and accuses you of being an imposter. Thus everyone wants to know why you did not say, in the first place, that you did not witness the accident. So now you are investigating the cost of plastic surgery.

These are the basic patterns for writing humor that brings a chuckle and lifts the daily cares. No doubt, you can use them to create new combinations.

Suggested Practice

Test your sense of humor and do a slant and a work sheet on any one of the humor patterns. Before you do the first draft, write your illustrations for the factual patterns and block out the scenes or substitutes for the fictional.

17.

How to Use
Transitions

Although the article consists of a number of separate units, these are tightly connected to give the impression of oneness. The devices of continuity are *transitions*. An article with good transitioning holds the reader's attention until he has read the last word. Transitions are divided into three groups.

STRINGING THE PARTS

You are already familiar with the red string, the single continuity which appears in all parts of the article and ties it together. There are a number of others which have been mentioned but not fully explained and are common to both types of articles with only slight variations.

1. *Capsule Sentence and Theme*

In most factual articles your best device and frequently the only one for transitioning is the capsule sentence. Each point for discussion, with its illustrations, expands the various facets of this general statement concerning your specific views on a subject. As you develop the article, you repeat portions of your capsule sentence or re-state the sentence in a different manner. This red string guides the reader through the article.

The capsule sentence is to the factual article what the theme is to the personal experience, nostalgic, and fictional humor articles. The theme summarizes the major character's change or the change of other characters to him. This change is always a result of action with other characters. When you open an article with theme, you state only part of it. As the action continues, you add bits until the climax when you state the complete theme.

The nostalgic example opens with theme, pointing out that Father believed in the possible. Mother calls it an impossible belief. In each scene, Father continues to practice the possible although it appears wild, unreasonable, improbable, and doomed to failure. In the climax, Mother explains practicing the possible as an impossible belief in the occurrence of the improbable.

2. *Single Emotion*

In your slant sheet you determine the emotional reaction of your reader. This emotional reaction remains the same as you move from point to point in the development of the factual patterns. If confidence is the emotion, each separate part builds this mood.

The fictional article gets a stronger emotional reaction from the reader than the factual. The emotion differs with each one, but the reaction you choose dominates the article. All action, characterization, beads of flashback, setting, and conflict reflect this single emotion.

The single emotion in the nostalgic example is humorously nostalgic. Admiration dominates the personality sketch. The single reader reaction in the first person experience is inspiration.

3. *Viewpoint*

Any time you write the article in the first person, the *I* ties the various parts together. Since these are your experiences which you share with the reader, you give unity to the article. The second person provides a similar unity, for the focus is on the reader. The implied viewpoint depends upon emotional impact for its continuity rather than simply the point of view.

4. *Illustrations*

When the illustrations of the factual patterns show people in the same walk of life and with the same purpose or goal as the reader, you are unifying your article. The danger here is that the illustrations appear too similar.

5. *Gimmick or Symbol*

Only the fictional articles utilize a gimmick or a symbol. A *gimmick* is any percept which the viewpoint character shares with the reader in regard to a person, place, or thing. The gimmick causes the trouble and helps to solve it. A love song, a family Bible, the smell of the ocean are all percepts which you can convert into gimmicks. The gimmick appears in each part of the article. The newspaper is the gimmick in the personality sketch and the cyclone cellar in the nostalgic piece.

When you endow a gimmick with a special, spiritual meaning, it becomes a *symbol*. If the viewpoint character feels he has good luck every time he carries a small knife in his pocket, he has endowed the gimmick with spiritual power. In the first person experience, the trailer symbolizes the life with Joe. The trailer ties the scenes together.

The reader must clearly understand the meaning of the symbol to the viewpoint character. If this is vague, you have lost the effectiveness of the transition. Introduce both the gimmick and the symbol in the critical situation. The gimmick appears in action articles while the symbol works better where characterization is important.

6. *Character Trait*

The character trait is one of the best devices for continuity in writing the fictional article. You show this same character trait in each part of the article. Character trait is strongest in the personality sketch, since the whole article is characterization. Ed Harvey's trait of practicing freedom of the press dominates the entire piece.

In the first person experience, the viewpoint character's determination to support herself and her family is the trait, but other transitions, such as symbol and viewpoint, give assistance. Father's faith in the fallen is the trait in the nostalgic piece, but the theme and the gimmick reinforce it. Two humor patterns, the personality sketch satire and the character trait formula, make their transitions chiefly with the trait.

7. *Setting*

The setting for action is often important in the how-to-do-it piece. You may need a workshop to construct the chest. The action in an idea article may revolve around the home while that in a controversial article centers in a school, church, or congress. Setting plays a supporting role.

When setting creates the conflict in the fictional article, this is the dominant red string. A typical example is a personal experience article relating a man's struggles against the forces of nature on a deserted island.

In most fictional articles, setting is only a supporting transition since all scenes use a basic area. The basic setting in the nostalgic piece is the home and backyard. The college campus comprises the basic setting in the personal experience article. In the personality sketch the newspaper office is implied as the setting.

8. *Motivation*

Motivation is a secondary transition in the factual article, and it suggests why you-the-author wrote the piece. You write the how-to-do-it and the idea articles to share your know-how and give the reader confidence to put your information into practice. The motivation behind the controversial piece is to convert readers to your way of thinking. The inspirational article wants to help the reader get rid of his "blues" or depressive feelings.

In the personality sketch, your motivation frequently is to let the person carry an important message to the reader. The example shows that freedom of the press does exist and is recognized by the world. The nostalgic piece is another carrier of a message—a helping hand is the difference between success and failure. Humor can also carry a message as well as offer pleasant escape.

The personal experience needs motivation to show how you-the-author became involved. Any time the past strongly motivates the present, the solid flashback is a good transitioning device. You write the flashback with strong dramatic words and picture phrases. In each new scene, you repeat a strong phrase or sentence to remind the reader and yourself of this motivation. Never repeat the entire flashback or add any new information. All information goes in this one solid flashback.

Write the flashback as a series of incidents, dramatic actions, emotional reminiscences, rapid narration, or a scene. The personal experience example needs a solid flashback to show why the viewpoint character was so determined to carry out Joe's wishes.

> That last day began like any other. I walked to the car with Joe as I always did. He leaned down and kissed me. *"Take care of my girls* and *give them a bushel of happiness."* He started to climb in the car, then stopped.
>
> "What's wrong?" *I was frightened.* He looked so strange.

"If anything should happen—this job has its danger-
ous moments." He tried to force a grin. "I know
you'll find a way to *give the girls an education,* to
carry out our plans for them."

"You know I will, but don't talk like that," I begged.
He laughed, then kissed me again as if *it were to
last forever.*

That was the last time I saw Joe alive.

The seven italicized parts will appear in various scenes to
remind the reader of the total motivation and to create
transitions in the experience. The personality sketch may
also require a flashback.

Every article relies on several devices to provide the red
string. Some are primary in that they appear in every article with this pattern. Others are secondary in that their
use is optional. The following table will serve as a quick
reference.

PATTERN	PRIMARY	SECONDARY
Informative	capsule sentence	numbered arrangement
How-to-do-it	capsule sentence you-viewpoint confidence emotion	numbered steps gimmick setting motivation
Idea	capsule sentence practical emotion	problem-solution arrangement viewpoint illustrations

		motivation setting
Controversial	capsule sentence logical emotion researched illustrations	motivation viewpoint setting
Inspirational	capsule sentence inspiring emotion trait of wrong image	viewpoint motivation illustrations
Personality sketch	trait capsule sentence	setting motivation of author and personality viewpoint gimmick or symbol
Personal experience	viewpoint trait theme	emotion motivation setting gimmick or symbol
Nostalgic	emotion theme	viewpoint setting trait motivation gimmick or symbol

HUMOR

Satire	same as pattern	same as pattern
Character trait	trait viewpoint	emotion setting motivation
Problem	problem viewpoint	gimmick or symbol theme

OVERLAPPING THE BREAKS

A factual article consists of points and illustrations while the fictional piece contains scenes and scene substitutes. These separate units automatically provide certain natural breaks in time, place, and emotion. These breaks offer the reader an opportunity to stop reading unless you overlap so that he is not aware of the shift.

1. *Time and Place*

In the fictional article each scene has a different time and usually another setting from the previous one. To interlock these, you mention the old time and imply the new one in the last line of the final paragraph of the scene. If the place changes, mention time and place. In the first sentence of the next scene, mention the new time and place before you begin the action.

> Father stood up from the *breakfast table* and ended the argument. "I must get to the bank. We can discuss it *tonight.*"
>
> Mother brought up the cellar business that *night* at *supper.*

The transitions are italicized. The beginner relates the boring details of the day, but the professional writer uses transitions to eliminate them and still keep the continuity of the action.

The factual article overlaps the point to develop with either the previous one or the capsule sentence. You alternate for variety. The illustration overlaps the point it illustrates, and, if possible, the previous illustration. You overlap the idea, the time, the place, or the character exactly as illustrated above.

2. *Emotion*

Since you have a break in scene or point to illustrate, you do not shift the emotion until the middle of the paragraph. While the article has a single dominant emotion, there are shades of intensity. The shades of anger are: smouldering, explosive, sarcastic, stunned, hurt, cool. So if you show anger as the dominant emotion, it varies from cool to raging as you develop the scenes or the points. These changes come in the middle of the paragraph or follow the *said* in dialogue.

> "Your very special friend, Mr. Faulkner, came by this afternoon," Mother said sweetly. Then her tone changed. "No person in his right mind would buy his worthless note, and you know it. He hasn't completed a construction job of any kind in ten years, much less a cyclone cellar."

Mother changes from sweetness to anger.

The emotion does not change with each paragraph but may run through several. You may argue several paragraphs, then concede before you attack.

3. *Points and Plants*

You *point* to an event before it happens; otherwise the

reader is shocked and may stop reading. In the nostalgic article, a pointer is the fact that Father bought the bad notes and let the debtor repay with service. Another pointer is Father's membership on the school board so he is aware of the mathematical ability of the teacher.

A *plant* is an object, a talent, or a group of people that appears later in the article. You plant a gimmick or a symbol. The rose garden is a plant in the nostalgic article and the tutor who married the daughter is one in the personal experience. You introduce a plant in one scene or in the point to develop, and pick it up in the next one.

To check these transition devices, read the last sentence of the old part and the first of the new section. Do they overlap? Trace the emotional line and make sure the shift comes within the paragraph. If you underline each point and plant, it is easy to see if you have followed through.

Erasing the Paragraphs

Paragraphing offers the reader a convenient stopping point. Although you need the paragraphs for forward movement, each must lead right into the next. The solution is simple. The transition device appears in the last line of one paragraph and the first sentence of the next. There are several devices which accomplish this.

1. *By Repetition*

You repeat the word or a similar one.

> So put your *complaints* in *writing*.
> A *written complaint* provides a record in the file.

Make a transition of the idea.

> Write *today*.
>   *Tomorrow* is too *late*.

Keep the same mood.

> Your best solution is to put a ban on your worries.
>   Refuse to worry about three days in the week: yesterday, today, and tomorrow.

Make the sentences the same length.

> So you were wrong.
>   You can be right.

Use the same sounds. Here is a repetition of contrasts.

> The telephone *trilled* through the *quiet* of the kitchen.
>   Mother *silenced* it on the third *high C*.

Keep the same rhythm. Both lines have the same flow in this illustration. Alliteration also creates rhythm.

> I rushed to mop up the overflow.
>   The exhausted appliance gasped for breath.

2. *By Comparison and Contrast*

The first part of the comparison or contrast appears in the last sentence of the paragraph. The second part or the completion comes in the first sentence of the new paragraph.

Most people know the general provisions of a guarantee.

Few people are acquainted with the hair-splitting ones in the fine print.

3. *By Familiar and Unfamiliar*

Plant the familiar at the end of one paragraph and move to the unfamiliar in the next, or reverse the process.

Most people in town used dugouts or holes in the ground for protection against cyclones.

The cellar, particularly one lined with cement and roofed with rock, was unheard of by everyone but Father and Mr. Faulkner.

4. *By the Reversal*

Let the paragraph wind up heading in one direction. The first sentence of the new paragraph reverses the thought.

"Our cellar will be the strongest, the largest, the—"

"One never completed," Mother finished for Father.

5. *By Connectives*

You are familiar with connectives: *consequently, therefore, as a result, nevertheless,* and others. They give smoothness to your factual copy, but do not rely on them entirely. These words are more popular as transitions for the formal essay.

To test your transitions between paragraphs, read the last sentence of one paragraph and the first of the next. Do they blend? If they don't, work on your transition. Transitioning, a part of revision and polishing, is a conscious process done when you have completed the first draft of your article.

SUGGESTED PRACTICE

When you have completed a first draft on any one of your ideas, begin your revision by checking the transitions.

18.

Planning
Your Work Schedule

Many new writers waste precious time because they do not know how to arrange a work schedule. Through experience and necessity, professional writers have learned to organize their working time for the most profitable production. Each writer must fit his writing into his daily routine, but most successful writers organize their time in this way.

THINKING TIME

A new writer spends too little time thinking through his idea and eagerly rushes to the typewriter to make a first draft which can lead only to numerous revisions. If you think best at the typewriter, then do so but do not plunge into a first draft. Follow these steps in thinking.

1. *Search for a Salable Idea*

Do not be satisfied with the first idea which pops into your head, but invest some effort to find several. Go through all of the sources suggested in Chapter 1 and list as many possible ideas as catch your enthusiasm. From this list select the one which pushes you to write.

2. *Test Your Idea*

Before you begin to work on this idea, carefully give it the six-way test explained in the opening chapter. If it does not pass, then test the next one and so on until you are satisfied.

3. *Make a Tentative Work Sheet*

Your first step in making a work sheet is to write several capsule sentences or themes stating your personal opinion in regard to the idea. From these, select the one which best expresses your personal reaction.

The way you state the capsule sentence or theme often leads you to the correct pattern. You may find that you need to combine two patterns to project your idea adequately. With the correct pattern in mind, go to work on the points to develop or the plot structure.

When you have listed all the points or complications you can think of in relation to the capsule sentence or theme, combine, re-state, or discard until you have from three to five strong statements or the minimum in scenes to develop the capsule sentence or theme. Place these on individual cards and sheets so you can shift them around to determine the best arrangement.

Your next step is to go to work on the illustrations or scenes, writing them on separate sheets of paper. Match these to the points for development or the plot formula. When you complete this, you are ready to do the slant sheet and then the pattern work sheet.

Thinking time includes finding the idea, testing it, doing a slant and a work sheet. As you become more adept in writing, you will learn to think through much of this process even before you begin the tentative work sheet at the typewriter. At lunch, waiting in the dentist's office, or commuting, your mind will work actively on your idea.

RESEARCH TIME

While you are thinking about your idea, you may need more information. The more research you do on an idea, the easier will come the organization. You will do two types of research.

1. *On the Market*

As soon as you have chosen your idea, you will want to check it immediately in the *Reader's Guide* at the library. This research shows how much has been written on the subject and in what magazines. If the magazines are available, read them.

To this market information, add that from professional journals for writers. They contain information on needs of editors as to subject, treatment, length, and pay. In some of these magazines, the editor urges the writer to read certain outstanding articles in current issues. By all means study them. If you are not acquainted with the magazines listed, read and analyze them.

When you submit an article to an editor, sometimes he will send you an analysis sheet of the type of article he desires. A few editors have printed booklets on how to write for them. You can, however, compile the same information by analyzing six issues of his magazine.

Begin your analysis by reading all the articles backward, the last paragraph first, then the next to the last, and so on until you have finished it. This way you will clearly see the structure, and the emotional impact or the expert polishing job will not lead you astray while you analyze the article.

To picture the reader of the magazine clearly, study the advertisements, the letters to the editor, the fillers, or short pieces contributed by readers. The editorial page, staff written articles, and market reports in professional writing journals picture the editor.

Some articles are seasonal. If you study the table of contents of a magazine for three years you will discover that articles run in cycles. April issues usually carry an article on cancer, June on brides or graduation, and September on back to school. You submit seasonal articles six months ahead for some publications and three for others.

When you have researched the market, revise your slant sheet. Selecting the right market is a combination of finding out what the editor has bought in the past, what he wants to buy now, and what research facilities you have available.

2. *Subject*

A new writer frequently selects a subject which requires costly research facilities. When a writer becomes established or works on special assignment, the editor provides additional pay on occasions calling for extensive research. As a beginner, you have no choice but to hold your research cost to a minimum.

Your research may include the secondary sources or material already published by others on file at your public library. The chief danger here is that you may end up by re-hashing what has already been said with the same old slant. If there is no new data on the subject, give up the idea for the present if it will release its grip on you.

Try to find a way to do original research. Most articles require original research through interviews or going to the original sources of published material, such as letters or documents. If these sources are within a short distance of your home, make use of them.

3. *Query Letter*

When you know the slant of the market and have done enough research to make the final work sheet, you may want to query the editor in regard to a factual article on the subject. Before you write the article, you can find out if the editor has already scheduled such an article or if it is not the type he wants. He will not promise to buy from your query, but he will agree to look at it on speculation.

Some writers prefer to send the editor a work sheet including the hook, the capsule sentence, the authority, the points for development, one completely written illustration to show style of writing, the conclusion, and the twist. Others use a brief query letter. The first paragraph is the hook, the next asks if the editor would be interested in an article dealing with this subject and developed in this way. You may illustrate one of the points, suggest the possibility of pictures or charts, and mention any specialized experience.

The query letter indicates that you are familiar with the subject and have plenty of material. Especially do you want to show that you know how to organize and illustrate the material with anecdotes, pictures, or charts. If the material is seasonal, you can let the editor know how soon you can deliver the article. The query letter is your sales pitch, so work on it.

Each query letter differs in content for each article since it must showcase the idea. You will also change the slant when you send to a different editor. Here is an example of a query letter for the guarantee idea slanted for the digest market.

> 916 Oak Street
> Dallas, Texas
> May 21, 19—

Editor
Non-Fiction
Fifth Avenue
New York City

Dear Sir:

Guarantees are issued for the protection of the buyer, but a large percentage of people pay for their own repairs rather than risk an argument over replacements.

This is a false assumption, for most companies are willing to stand behind their guarantees if you use the right approach.

Are you interested in seeing an article which discusses the right approach to using a guarantee? It will cover such situations as the unquestionable complaint, the unwritten guarantee, the doubtful interpretation, the stubborn resistance, and the unexpected replacement.

For the past ten years I have used guarantees on approximately thirty products varying from cars to bridge cards. Furthermore, I have encouraged my friends to use guarantees; consequently I have numerous first-hand experiences to illustrate the proposed article. The length will be around 1800 words.

May I hear from you?

Sincerely yours,

At one time, beginners were not too successful with a query, for editors preferred to see the style of writing. With more and more unsolicited manuscripts pouring in for the editor, he now suggests that the writer send a query. As a beginner, you may find the complete work sheet is more successful. Once an editor has bought several articles from you, then you send him the query letter.

Any article which depends on style of writing is not a subject of query. Included in this group are: inspirational, nostalgic, personal experience, and humor. Because the informative article is a compilation of known facts, it is better to send the article. A query works well for how-to-do-it, idea, controversial, and personality sketch.

4. *Final Research*

While you are writing your first draft, you probably will

discover that you need more information on certain points. Take a red pencil and put an *x* in the margin. When you complete the draft, do all the research at one time. After you submit your article to an editor, he may request more elaboration, so save all your notes.

TYPEWRITER TIME

When you have thoroughly thought through your idea and completed the necessary research, you are ready to put your work sheet into the first draft. This is typewriter time.

1. *The First Draft*

No one can tell you when to do your typewriter time, but most writers prefer the morning hours when the mind is fresh. You do limit your typewriter time on a first draft to not more than four or five pages. Some days you may do these in a matter of an hour while on others you will put in eight hours. Make it a rule never to leave your typewriter until you have completed your quota.

If you finish in a short time, go back over what you have written with an eye to improving it, or plan what you will do the next day. Each day re-read what you wrote previously so you will continue in the same mood. Do not polish!

2. *The Final Draft*

No one can tell you how many drafts you will do on an article. You will keep revising and polishing until you think you are satisfied. Even then, after you drop it in the mail box, you wish you could take it back and do more work.

Setting a quota of pages does not apply to any draft other than the first. You work at revision until you are tired. Do something else, possibly with your hands. This change of duties relaxes you, and you are ready to go back to the revision. Regardless of whether it is a first or final draft, always make a carbon. A comparison of the two convinces you of the improvement and relieves your worries that you have worked the sparkle from the piece.

There is a certain form to follow in typing the final draft:

Your name
Street address
Town, State

Approximately
1800 words

THE TITLE IN CAPITALS
by Your Name

Come down about one-third of a page for the title. Skip three spaces after your name and indent ten from the margin for the first line of each paragraph. Leave a one-inch margin on all sides of the page. Number the first page in the center at the bottom.

On each succeeding page, use your last name and a key word from the title in the upper left-hand corner. Number the page three spaces down on the right-hand side.

Boggess (Key word)

2

(Begin copy about three spaces down from the number.)

On the last page put "The End," then repeat your name and address three spaces down and against the left-hand margin.

If you want to use a title sheet, put the title of the article and your name in the center of the page. Send the manuscript without a letter unless the subject deals with a specialized experience. If you wrote on flying planes, you want to let the editor know that you are a commercial pilot. Writers differ on the question of binding a manuscript. If you do wish to bind it, use a plain cover with fastenings on the left-hand margin.

Type your manuscript on good white bond paper of standard size (8½ × 11) which does not rumple easily or tear. Type it double spaced, and be sure the ribbon is dark and the type clean.

3. *Mailing*

Any manuscript which runs more than three pages is mailed flat. Equip yourself with two sizes of manila envelopes so that you can include one with postage and addressed to yourself for the return trip if the manuscript is rejected. Send it either first class or at educational rates. With the rising cost of postage, most writers use the educational material rate. Card-board in the envelope saves much retyping.

Some writers worry about their manuscripts' reaching the editor. Many editors have a form postal card which notifies you of the arrival of the manuscript. For your own peace of mind, include with your manuscript a postal card addressed to yourself saying the editor has received the manuscript.

SIMMERING TIME

As soon as you finish the first draft, you are convinced that you have written nothing but "pearls of wisdom." If you put it aside for a week or two, you become more objective and can see any number of ways to improve the piece. Simmering time includes revision and polishing. The difference between a beginner and a professional is revision.

1. *Revision*

While most writers work out their own system for revision, a good procedure is to re-check your work sheet. The more thought you put into organizing your idea, the less revision you need to do.

For the factual article, you proceed in this manner:

HOOK: Will another type be better? Does it state your general subject and hint at the specific slant?

CAPSULE SENTENCE: Have you stated this as well as you can? Is it clear cut and does it express the message you want to give the reader?

AUTHORITY: Have you assured the reader that you know your subject? Is your authority free of egotism and bias? Have you used the best method to show your authority?

DEVELOPMENT: Have you used the best pattern for your development? Do you have the best arrangement of your points? Do you have too many or too few? Do you use too many subheads?

Are the illustrations the best you can provide? Do they elaborate the point? Are they varied in regard to devices? Have you varied the location in relation to the point to prove?

CONCLUSION: Is it too long? Does it sum up the subject or offer a constructive plan, if required? Does it relate to the capsule sentence? Is the mood the same?

TWIST: Does it relate to the hook in mood and subject? Is it too long? Does it touch the reader?

In the fictional article, here is the approach:

PATTERN: Have you selected the best pattern? Are the scenes in the proper sequence? Is the dialogue cycle the best you can write? Does it move the action forward? Is there a choice of action at the end of each scene? Do you set the time and place? Are there too few or too many scenes?

CHARACTERIZATION: Do you have the correct viewpoint? Do you have the right traits and motivation for the characters? Do you establish a negative and affirmative trait for the major character? Does the character change fit these traits and the action in the article? Does the change fit the problem and the motivation? Is the change established at the end? Does the theme correctly summarize the change? Is this the theme you wished to prove? Have you developed both the inner and outer conflict? Do all characters function?

You will probably think of other key questions to ask yourself. In fact, you will soon spot your weakness in writing and learn to look for it immediately. Perhaps the decision points are weak, or you anti-climax the crisis with complications which are too strong.

2. *Polishing*

While revision corrects the structural defects in an article, polishing gives the manuscript the stamp of the professional. You start with the first sentence and work on your choice of words, the structure of the sentence, and the mood projected. If the article is too long, you cut scientifically.

In the factual article, cut out a point and an illustration or combine with another if you need to cut several hundred words. When less than a hundred, cut a word here and there, adjectives and adverbs.

Cutting the fictional article begins with any paragraph of straight description which does not advance the plot, or with any unnecessary flashback. Combine functions to eliminate a character. Cut a whole scene or either combine it with another or reduce it to a series of incidents. Wordiness creeps into dialogue more than any other place, so be sure each speech advances the plot action.

In the event that the factual article is too short, which rarely occurs, add another point or more illustrations. When you expand the fictional article, put the extra wordage on characterization for stronger conflict. Blow up a scene substitute into a full scene.

Learn early to use the tape treatment in cutting or expanding an article. If you are cutting out a scene or point in the development, take your scissors and remove it. Tape the remaining parts together. If you insert, cut apart and tape it in place. This will save hours of typing and will keep you polishing only those parts which need it. Polishing is spot revision to smooth out only the rough places.

With the cutting or expanding completed, check the transitions as directed in the previous chapter. For a final polish, read the manuscript for punctuation, spelling, and grammar. No one can tell you how many readings you will give each manuscript. Each article is a different case.

REFUELING TIME

Some writers live in constant fear of "going dry." This is an unnecessary worry if you refuel each day.

1. *Notebook*

The new writer thinks he has so many ideas that he will never run out, but he does, quite quickly. So, to assure yourself that you will not run dry, keep a little notebook handy to jot down title, characters, conversations, or ideas of any kind. At times you wake up in the middle of the night with a terrific idea! Get up and record it, or you will forget by morning. Never trust your memory, even in the day time.

2. *File Box*

Transfer the items from your notebook to a file box. You may set aside a certain time or do it as your notebook becomes too full. Arrange the items alphabetically, by subject, or any other way which suits you. You may also use this file box to hold your submittal cards showing when you sent the manuscript, where, and the results.

Attach the rejection slips to this card or to the carbon of the manuscript. Rejection slips speak a language which you must learn. All magazines have a standard one which states they can not use your manuscript. This does not mean it is not salable.

Frequently, the editor will write you a note on the rejection slip and point out a defect. By all means follow this suggestion. The editor may even sign his name to the slip. When you submit again, send the manuscript to this editor. Sometimes he sends the editorial requirements.

Editors have a more encouraging rejection slip which is also printed but has a place to type in your name and another for the editor to sign. This one will state that the manuscript does not fit their needs, but they would like to see more of your work. Keep sending to this editor.

The best type of rejection is a personal letter from the editor pointing out where the manuscript needs revision. He may or may not suggest that you do the revision and send it back. Another form of encouragement is a check sheet listing defects that appear in the manuscript. These also are signed.

When your manuscript has been to six markets, check

your rejection slips, the length of time each editor kept it, which can indicate the interest, and any suggestions for revision. Do more research on market requirements of the editor who gave you the most encouragement.

3. *Folder*

Whether you realize it or not, you store your ideas in your subconscious when you put them in a notebook or transfer them to a card for your file box. The first thing you know, you will think of something to add to this basic idea. When you reach this stage, take the card out of the box and put it in a folder with a tentative title.

From time to time, you will think of an illustration or a point, a possible capsule sentence or title. Type these and drop them in the folder. Keep at least ten ideas germinating. As soon as you pull one from your file to put into a work sheet, replace it with another from your file box.

4. *Dead File*

Don't ever throw away an idea you have sold as an article, but put it in the dormant file. One day you will think of a fresh approach or find some new material which will make it an entirely different article. Make a practice of going through the file cards or the carbons of the article periodically. You will always have an abundance of ideas as long as you constantly refuel from a notebook, file box, and folder.

A FINAL WORD

You are probably wondering why you have not figured out all of these fundamentals of writing for yourself. Very few people do, for this clinical approach to writing represents the combined experiences of a large number of professional writers as well as testing the method on students in writing classes for ten years. Understanding these fundamentals is only the first step.

Making these techniques work for you is the second, and is not easy. This analytical approach to writing requires discipline. At first, you must force yourself to apply the techniques to anything and everything you write. One day you will write too emotionally and the next too flatly. Eventually, the professional technique will help you find the right balance, and the process becomes automatic.

In learning to write professionally, you recognize only one competitor—yourself. Never let the sales of others upset or discourage you. Your goal is to make the copy you do today better than that you did yesterday.

The only "black magic" which changes you into a selling writer is to work consistently and persistently to apply these professional techniques to every piece you write. These are all the tools you need to write a salable article.

As soon as you complete one article, send it to the first editor on your market list. Go to work immediately on a new one. If you continue this routine, one day soon a check will arrive in the mail. Then you can proudly proclaim, "I know how to write an article that sells."

Index

Index